T0245996

GLIMMER

GLIMMER

A Story of Survival, Hope, and Healing

KIMBERLY SHANNON MURPHY

With Genevieve Field

Foreword by Cameron Diaz

HARPER WAVE

An Imprint of HarperCollins*Publishers*

HarperCollins books may be purchased for educational, business, or sales promotional use. For information, please email the Special Markets Department at SPsales@harpercollins.com.

Foreword © 2023 by Cameron Diaz

FIRST EDITION

Designed by Bonni Leon-Berman

Library of Congress Cataloging-in-Publication Data has been applied for.

ISBN 978-0-06-322826-9

23 24 25 26 27 LBC 5 4 3 2 1

AUTHOR'S NOTE

THIS IS A WORK OF nonfiction. The events and experiences detailed herein are all true and have been faithfully rendered as I have remembered them, to the best of my ability. Some names and some identifying details and circumstances have been changed in order to protect the integrity and/or anonymity of the various individuals involved. The timing of some events has been compressed for purposes of narrative flow. Though conversations come from my keen recollection of them, they are not written to represent word-for-word documentation; rather, I've retold them in a way that evokes the real feeling and meaning of what was said, in keeping with the true essence of the mood and spirit of the event.

For my
Aunt Pat-Tree-Sha,
the first one
to speak up

The unconscious wants truth, as the body does.

—Adrienne Rich, *On Lies, Secrets, and Silence:
Selected Prose 1966–1978*

CONTENTS

CONTENTS

Part III   LANDING

FOREWORD
by Cameron Diaz

You never know, when you meet someone, what they will mean to you—if they're simply a passing acquaintance, or if they will become a lifelong friend, someone who will impact your life in ways you can't yet imagine. When I met Kimberly fifteen years ago, she was introduced to me as my stunt double for a movie I was filming. When I shook her hand, I had no idea that I was meeting one of the great teachers of my life, a woman who, time and time again, has consistently shown me by example what true strength and courage look like.

The Kimberly I met all those years ago is still, in many ways, the Kimberly I know today—equal parts kind and determined, fierce and vulnerable. But the truth is that I have also watched her evolve in radical ways over the course of our friendship. I have watched as she acknowledged a traumatic past, and fought for her very survival. I have watched as she wrote and rewrote her own narrative, always asking herself, *Am I in the right place? Am I improving myself? Am I finding my purpose?* And I have watched as she forged a new path for her life, one that comes with profound challenges but also profound opportunities for growth and healing.

Of course, none of us are immune to suffering in this lifetime; pain is a part of the deal in this wild ride we take as human beings. But there is some suffering that truly tests the limits of our capacity. When Kimberly first shared her story with me, I was not only shocked by what she had endured, I was also shocked by how she had managed to thrive while living with the deep physiological imprint of trauma. I was in awe of her spirit, of her strength, of her instinct for survival. Here was a woman who had endured unspeakable abuse—I would go so far as to call it pure evil—and yet, she was determined to find growth in her pain. On her journey to heal, she has continually overcome every obstacle thrown at her, torn down every wall put in place to limit her. As an adult—and now a parent herself—she has actively chosen to give herself the kind of security and safety she lacked as a child. And now, she is extending that safety to others.

Kimberly has wanted to write a book for as long as I've known her. Over the years, she's shared pieces of her writing with me, as she began to tell her story page by page, hoping it one day would become a resource that could help others. I have watched this project grow and evolve in tandem with Kimberly's healing journey. Writing this book has been no easy feat for her. We had many phone calls through her process, as she excavated her past, worked through the pain, and put her story on paper. Along the way, she also reached out to every major trauma doctor in the field. Without fail, she was able to not only connect with them, but learn from them, and then transmute that knowledge into the experiences she shares here.

Today you hold in your hands a survivor's story. This book is so much more than the sum of its parts. It is a gift. It is Kimberly's offering to readers suffering in silence. It is a companion for anyone who has endured trauma, at any level. And it is a beautiful tribute to the strength and power of the human spirit.

Whoever you are, whatever life has put in your path, I hope that reading Kimberly's story serves as a conduit to healing. No matter who has tried to capture your spirit or how hopeless you may feel, it is never too late to speak your truth, to reclaim your power, and to transform your pain into purpose. I believe that the flame of hope can be nurtured in even our darkest moments. That it is within all of us to prevail from trauma we have suffered. All we need is a glimmer to know what is possible.

GLIMMER

PROLOGUE

Splinter by splinter, the medic tweezes candy glass from my face. I don't mind the stinging. I don't flinch. My heart is beating slowly now. My body is contained in the tight skin of my motion capture suit. All around me in the cavernous warehouse where we're filming *I Am Legend*, people are freaking out. The stunt coordinator is huddled with the rigging crew in charge of my descender. The first AD crouches at my feet: "Oh my God, are you *sure* you're okay?"

Ten minutes ago, I did a high fall through a glass window. We'd done everything right, just like in rehearsals, which went perfectly. But this time, my wire didn't stop me five feet above the ground like it was supposed to; I flew past my end mark, landing face-first in a pile of broken shards.

The stunt coordinator is insisting that I go to the ER, but I shake my head and repeat calmly, so they will take me seriously, "No, I'm not going to the hospital. I want to do it again." Then I return to studying my shredded-up palms. I could be meditating on my yoga mat, I feel so centered. I close my eyes and imagine I'm an ancient stone statue, damaged by the elements but still whole.

When the medic is finished pressing dozens of tiny Band-Aids over the cuts, I find the makeup artist. *Tsk*-ing as she works, she does her best to reaffix the hot pink motion capture dots that were washed from my face with all the blood and hydrogen peroxide.

"I've never seen anyone work in this condition before," she says, shaking her head. "If you weren't playing a creature, it would never work." What she means is we're all lucky I'm not doubling for the beautiful lead actress on this one. I'm playing a monster, so it's okay that I look like one. When she thinks I'm not paying attention, I catch the makeup artist mouthing, *What the fuck?* in the mirror to the mortified assistant who waits to lead me back to set. They think I'm crazy, but I feel proud. It's acceptable to wear my pain on the outside here. My blood shows my toughness, my resiliency. They actually pay me to do this.

We do the stunt three more times. I hear: "We got that. Cut. Print. That's lunch."

Quietly, I approach the stunt coordinator and ask if it's okay to get stitched up now.

"Uh, *yeah!*" he says. "I've been trying to get you to go all day."

———

I find myself returning to the set that evening. My skin is a sunset of bruises, my right eye is nearly swollen shut, and stitches zigzag across my face. I really am a creature now.

"Kimberly, what are you doing here?" everyone asks.

"Just making sure you don't need me!" I say, enjoying the alarm in their voices.

It hits me, with thudding obviousness, that I'm lying. I'm fully aware that my work is done for the day. I've come back to set because the connective tissue between my present and my past is poking through again. Instead of worrying, like any normal person would, that I'll be scarred for life, I'm exuberant, parading my injuries. Like I used to, when I was cutting. *Look! My outsides match my insides! See what I can survive?*

Fuck. Time to go back to therapy.

Three years into my career as a stuntwoman, I thought I was over *wanting* to get hurt on the job so I could feel the power-high of "handling" it. I thought I'd transcended the inner programming of my past. I was done letting him win, done with all the crying out. I thought being successful at work meant I was okay now.

The thing about incest: it messes with your mind and makes you forget who you are, who you were, and what you were meant for in this world. You can spend your whole life trying to imagine: *Who would I be, if they'd never put their hands on me?*

Part I

SPLITTING

LONG BEFORE I HAD MY memories, I had my dolls. I collected them, or more like they collected me. Every birthday, Mom gave me a Denise or Anna or Rebecca lying in a little pink coffin box with a cellophane lookout window. They were porcelain, expensive for us. Each came with a birth certificate, though some weren't given proper names, just labels—Irish Beauty, Victorian Style Doll, Lovely Girl on Swing. . . . I propped them on plastic stands on my dresser, and there they stood for years, wide-eyed and never resting in their hoopskirts and fairy gowns and communion dresses. I didn't play with them like my plastic Kimberly Cheerleader doll. I cared for and protected them, dusting their ringlets and petticoats every week. I think I envied them for getting to be pretty and also safe. Still we were a lot alike—perfect on the outside, hollow on the inside. We had bodies but no free will; histories we couldn't speak of but carried in our fibers. So much of me was missing then; so little made sense.

To show you my childhood, I will not fill in the blank spots, the holes where the memories fell through, even sometimes as they formed. The spaces between the words are the explanations I didn't have, the world as I felt it.

1

EIGHTIES
PARTIES

Parties were what the Tylers—Mom's side—did best. When there was something to celebrate, you didn't have to have a real conversation. With corks to pop or rugs to cut or songs to sing, it was just so easy to unknow what, way deep down, you knew.

...

Anniversary Party, 1983
Six years old

August in Oceanside. I close my window to the breeze. I like being sealed up. Every birthday and Christmas, I ask for curtains to hang around my four-poster bed, but it's too expensive. Except for my Lois Greenfield dance calendar and my dolls, my room is bare. Everything about our half Cape house on Skillman Avenue is practical and plain, like Mom. For a long time, we didn't have many pictures up. Then Grandpapa gave us a bunch of old maps, which Dad hung in the playroom with pushpins. I liked it better before.

There are exceptions to Mom's practicality. For parties, church, and dinners with her parents at Earle Avenue, she curls our hair and lines her eyes in shimmery turquoise like Princess Diana. Collette and I wear bows and scratchy dresses, sometimes even hats and corsages. If my grandparents call us *pretty* or *beautiful*, Mom is a success, and everything's alright. If Grandma Gen greets me with, "Kimberly, have you been doing cartwheels?" Mom will look stricken. Being perfect is the glue that holds her together, which holds us all together.

For the anniversary party, I'm taking a rare stand. I've put on my favorite, most protective blue skirt, with big front pockets to hide my restless hands and the hair elastics I'll snap against my fingers if I need to. The skirt has an attached wrap belt that I'm winding twice around my waist, so tight that I immediately have a stomachache. That's how I know it's tight enough.

"Mom says you're not wearing that," Dad informs me, appearing in my doorway. "She says we're doing a family portrait. To put on the other one." His Long Island accent is thicker and rougher than Mom's—*weah*, not *wear*, and *doin'*, not *doing*.

"It itches," I say, tightening the buckles on my Mary Janes. *And the shiny red sash makes him look*, I don't add.

"You think I like wearing this thing your mother puts me into? Kim, look at me."

Dad's hair, blond as mine in summer, is wet from the shower, but he's already sweating through his faded wedding-baptism-funeral suit, and his big neck is splotching red under his collar. He looks as uncomfortable as I always feel.

I briefly consider cooperating to make his life easier, but then I remember: once we get to the party, Dad will go to the bar and forget all about his suit, and me.

"I'm not changing," I say, reknotting my belt.

Dad sighs, twists his Marine Corps ring. His hands, big as baseball mitts, are scarred and calloused from being a mason his whole life. "It's just a dress, Kim," he says, patting his pocket where his Marlboro Reds should be. "It doesn't matter."

Sometimes I wonder if Dad even lives in the same world as us. Nothing is just anything at a Tyler party. Nothing is what it looks like. A dress can be your armor, or make you invisible, or make you pretty. Pretty girls can't disappear.

Mom is upset that the clothing argument made us late. She carries my little sister, Collette, on her hip and tugs me across the Rockville Links lawn with her free hand. Dad strides ahead in a stream of smoke, our store-wrapped gift tucked under his arm. I'm worried he'll drop it, and break Mom, too. I helped choose the crystal candy bowl at Macy's, watched her pick it up and look at the price tag and put it down and walk away and turn back and pick it up and put it down and finally rush it to the cash register before she could change her mind again.

On the clubhouse stairs, under a HAPPY 40TH ANNI-VERSARY banner, stands Grandpapa in his pin-striped suit, drinking with the men from his architecture firm. He sees us and does his tap-dancer trot down the stairs. Grandpapa personally greets every guest, even the late ones.

Dad shakes Grandpapa's hand, and Mom leans in with Collette so Grandpapa can kiss them. "Happy anniversary, Dad." She straightens the red rosebud on his lapel. "Where's Mom?"

"Oh, putting her lips on, I'm sure," replies Grandpapa. I smell the Old Spice he keeps on his dresser. *A white tin bottle with a red ship. A blue towel around his hips.* Shaking my head, I rub the toes of my Mary Janes together, soothing myself.

Mom lets go of my hand, gives the back of my neck a little squeeze.

"Hi, Grandpapa," I say.

His eyes cut to me—my sheer lace sleeves; my red sash; the short, ruffled hem of the white lace dress I wore, in the end, deciding it wasn't worth the battle. Deciding wrong.

"How's my prettiest granddaughter?" Grandpapa says. And the world just stops.

At the kids' table, my cousin Amanda and I play tic-tac-toe on the place mats. She takes bites between her Xs, but I push my plate away. Under the tablecloth, I bend my knee and jam the heel of my shoe into my crotch to tell my bladder STOP, don't GO. Bathrooms aren't safe at parties. Does everyone else know that, too, and go anyway? Is everyone braver than me? I've never asked Mom because I know what she'll say: "You're big enough to go alone; it's just family here!"

But Aunt Pat—my favorite aunt—will take me. I scan the crowded room for her, as the grown-ups break into another round of applause. They're toasting my grandparents, telling all the stories. About how Grandpapa always knows the right thing to do, and Grandma Gen always wears lipstick, even in a snowstorm. Most stories revolve around parties. And every single one has the same hero: Grandpapa.

Uncle Chris tells the one about the wedding where a drunk guest was causing a scene and Grandpapa went up behind him, whispered in his ear: "You don't want to ruin such a lovely day, do you?" He escorted the man outside, saving the day.

Dad stands up, raising his beer. "To Gen and Ed."

"To Gen and Ed!" shout the grown-ups.

"When I married Kath," Dad continues, "I felt so, so lucky. Not only was I marrying a wonderful woman, but I was marrying into the perfect family. For a kid from the other side of the tracks, it was something—the beautiful house, the beautiful cars. It was intimidating, alright. But you took me in as one of yours, and there's just no . . . no better family."

I press and wriggle in my chair, peeking over at Pop-pop and Grandma. Dad's parents are sitting right there at his table. Both are smiling, but I wonder if it hurts their feelings when Dad talks like he does. No one worships Grandpapa more than Dad. Mom says they have a special bond as war veterans. Grandpapa was a fighter pilot in World War II, and Dad was a minesweeper in Vietnam, but Mom says what they went through is the same underneath.

———

For the first anniversary portrait, it's just the Tylers—Grandpapa and Grandma Gen with their six kids: Mom, Aunt Pat, Daphne, Kristy, Chris, and Jon.

Next, the rest of us are called over. I prance and hop in place while Mom fluffs my bangs.

"Kim!" she whispers. "Run to the bathroom!"

"But I don't have to go!" I lie.

"Pick a lap, any lap, grandkids!" says the photographer.

I don't mind when Collette jumps on Mom. I have Aunt Pat. "Hey, pen pal." She pulls me onto her lap. Wrapped in her long, strong arms, her feather earrings tickling my cheek, I feel safe for the first time all day.

"Say rubies, everyone!"

"Rubieeees!"

My picture smile stays glued to my face as a wet snake slithers down my thigh. I'm peeing on Aunt Pat! Tears bristling, I bury my face in her neck. "*I'm sorry*," I whisper.

She squeezes me, dries my cheek with her hand. "Nothing to be sorry for," she says softly, into my hair. And I believe her. I know Aunt Pat cares more about me than her best silk pants. Being perfect is not what holds us together, love is.

...

Christmas Party, mid-eighties

Christmas steals Mom's energy, too. She doesn't even have enough to wrap our presents, just leaves them on the couch for us to "open" Christmas morning. Right cushion, Kimberly; left, Collette. Dad goes downstairs first, so he can howl, "Girls, we've been robbed!" Then we race each other down and have the good part of Christmas. I always get a new doll, and Collette gets books. There's no church because we do it on Christmas Eve. We have bacon and eggs and stay in our pajamas until it's time to get ready for the party. And that's the end of the good part.

Grandma Gen and Grandpapa have hosted the Christmas party since Mom was a kid. Every year, Earle Avenue turns into a Disney holiday–special house—its pointy eaves lined with colored lights, logs crackling in the fireplace, and tinsel dripping from everything in sight. To complete the picture, each time the doorbell rings, the guests in their red-and-green finery rush to the entryway to belt out a new round of "We Wish You a Merry Christmas." Grandpapa sings barbershop, my great-aunts play show tunes, and couples dance the Lindy. Grandpapa taught all his kids to ballroom dance, and they taught their husbands and wives, so everyone can fit the part. Meanwhile, the grown-ups drink and drink until the party splits into two parties, theirs and ours. Only ours isn't really a party, it's more like killing time.

My cousin Mike and I take turns sliding down the banister while we wait for them to wake up from their dreamworld and take us home. We whoosh down on our stomachs, tiptoe back up, and go again. We don't let my cousin Amanda go because she's the littlest and we're in charge.

"Keep a lookout for Grandma Gen," Mike orders his little sister. "Just sit on the bottom stair, and if she comes, say, 'Hi, Grandma Gen!'—loud, so we hear."

"But I don't *want* to sit at the bottom!" Amanda stomps, dangling her Christmas Barbie by the hair.

Secretly, I don't blame her. I wouldn't want to sit down there, either. The cuckoo clock hangs at the bottom of the stairs. It's the worst of all Grandpapa's clocks. They're everywhere: a grandfather on the middle landing and little ones in wood-and-metal frames ticking and chiming all over the house. Also, the blue bathroom is down there. The light is off, and the door is cracked open.

Mike caves and stations Amanda by the grandfather clock, where she'll never see Grandma Gen coming in time. We continue the game anyway, until her red talons reach up from below and snatch Mike off the railing. We're sent to the basement, like I knew we would be.

At least Grandma Gen won't come down here. The basement is Grandpapa's space, always freezing cold. It has red tile floors, a woodshop, a shiny black piano that plays all by itself, and a bar where he keeps only beer and cocktail stirrers. Mike likes to play bartender, but I stay away from there. In the corner of the room is the worktable with a pegboard on the wall that holds Grandpapa's tools. Each saw and hammer and screwdriver is outlined with a Sharpie, so it stays exactly in its place.

"Kimberly, there's glitter!" says Amanda, crouching over the wood scrap box. We're foraging through the pieces, elbows knocking, sawdust flying, when the doorbell rings upstairs. The ceiling rumbles with footsteps and "We wish you a merry CHRISTmas" begins and my cousins drop their wood bits and race upstairs to join the chorus. *Run! Follow them!*

screams my brain, but my feet don't move. They know I'm supposed to stay. I turn back to the table and get to work. I could never *create* down here, I just like the glue—sticking and unsticking and regluing and sticking and unsticking and regluing until I'm in a trance when, quietly, the door opens. I don't have to look up to know who's come.

Sometime—minutes, hours?—later, I slowly climb the basement stairs, a heavy presence following behind me. Past the blue bathroom, we enter the kitchen, Grandpapa and I. The room feels too bright, like I'm walking into the sunshine after a movie matinee. I put up my hand to shield my eyes, squinting. Some ladies washing dishes turn to stare. What do they see? I touch a swelling bump on my forehead, look down at my rumpled burgundy dress. My knees are bleeding through my ripped tights. They were brand-new for the party. Mom skipped her November manicure to afford them, and now look at what I've done.

Grandpapa is spick-and-span in his suit jacket and red tie. "Running in her stocking feet!" I hear him say, distantly, through my force field. "Tripped on a toy!"

I don't remember tripping on a toy. I don't remember anything.

He cracks a tray of ice into a Ho HO HO! tea towel, holding it out to me. "Keep this on that bump," he says. The way the women glance and blush you'd think he was Harrison Ford or something.

I'm so cold, always so cold around him. I don't want to

touch his ice. I just want to find my Kimberly doll. I left her alone in the living room, and she's probably scared.

Grandpapa rattles the sack. "Oh, Kimberly?" his voice is singsongy, teasing. "You aren't afraid of a little ice, are you?"

"Go on, dear!" the ladies chime in.

Nothing ever ends until the grown-ups win, so I reach through my force field and take the stupid ice.

"Thank you, Grandpapa."

Satisfied, the women turn back to their washing.

None of them questioned Grandpapa's story.

No one ever questions Grandpapa, period.

What's wrong with me that I do?

He must be right: I was all amped up on sugar, I went too fast.

Yes, I decide. It happened like that.

•••

Engagement Party, 1985
Eight years old

One December, we fly to California for a rare family trip. Aunt Pat is throwing Aunt Kristy an engagement party. Both of them live in Marin now. Aunt Kristy I don't know well enough to miss much. With her tight silk blouses, glittery brown eyes, and curly black hair that bounces even when she's standing still, she's as glamorous and intimidating as a fashion model.

I just want to see Aunt Pat, and the new house she shares with Aunt Shawn, who isn't an aunt by blood or marriage but has been best friends with Aunt Pat for so long she's part of the family. For weeks, I've been crossing off the squares on my calendar, imagining how the day will be. Aunt Pat and I will sneak away from the noisy party to the silent redwood grove she wrote about in her letter. We'll kneel under ferns taller than our heads and touch the smooth rocks in the icy stream, but I won't mind the cold because I'll be with Aunt Pat. No one at the party will notice I'm gone, and this time, I won't want them to.

But that's not how it's going to be—I know it as soon as we walk in the door. "Welcome, welcome!" Aunt Pat drifts from her kitchen, where all the cabinet doors are gaping open. She looks the same at first glance—tall and lean, short brown hair, dangly earrings, and a plain top with no bra underneath. But when she kneels to hug me, her smile doesn't fit on her face and she looks right past me. She reminds me of Mom, and this scares me. I don't want Aunt Pat to be like us. Aunt Pat is supposed to be different, strong and present, no matter what.

Dad whistles, throwing his arms wide. "Quite a place you got here, Pat!"

At home on Skillman Avenue, Dad slouches through the small rooms as if he's afraid of knocking them down. He doesn't have to do that here. Aunt Pat's house is big and open and bright like a museum, and seems to float in the trees. Each room opens into the next—no dark corners, no stairs. And it smells like Aunt Pat: incense and sage. My hands are just starting to relax in my yellow skirt pockets (a compromise) when Aunt Pat leads us through a sliding glass door.

On a sun-splattered deck, the whole extended Tyler family is yelling to be heard over "Sgt. Pepper." It's chaos out here. Aunt Kristy and Aunt Daphne, their hair salon-done, clutch Christmas envelopes and shriek into each other's streaky faces. An uncle snaps pictures as Grandpapa, in his favorite tasseled dress shoes, parts a chorus line to hand Mom her own envelope. They hug like wooden marionettes.

"What's happening?" I ask my cousin Mike.

"Grandpapa gave them five-thousand-dollar checks!"

"Oh!" I say, trying to feel the excitement. "Wow."

Mom shows her card to Dad, who slaps his forehead in a pantomime of amazement. I wrinkle my nose, then feel ungrateful and mean. It *is* a lot of money, and we don't have much—none of Grandpapa and Grandma Gen's kids are rich like them. I think they like it that way.

"When I'm Sixty-Four" comes on, and they all dance too fast. Mom does the time step, her breasts bouncing faster and faster under her flower-print dress. Grandma Gen, bedazzled from head to toe, pulls Grandpapa into the center of it all. Dipping her backward, he looks up, straight into me. The deck lurches under my feet.

I turn back inside. Down the tilting hall is a yellow bathroom with potted plants and a bubbly sky light. Checking behind me, I close myself into the warm sunny space, push the silver button on the knob: *click*. My hand hovers. Grandpapa and Grandma Gen have a rule: no locking doors, in case of fires. Even though we're not at their house, it's their rules we

follow, or that follow us. I twist the handle: *pop*. I lock it: *click*.
I'm beginning to sweat. *Pop* . . . *Click* . . . Neither way feels
safe. I untwist the lock.

One eye on the doorknob, I sit on the toilet, push down my
bobby socks, and run my fingers over my scabby ankles. The
bug bites are left over from summertime. I will never let them
heal; they're my security blanket that I take with me, everywhere. I pry one with my thumbnail, watching the blood rise,
letting down my guard.

It happens just like every other time: a creak; a crack in the
door; the red-ship smell; the tasseled dress shoes, stepping
through.

I'm on my feet, yanking down my skirt, by the time I
hear . . .

Click. "Came to check on you," he says. "Make sure you
didn't fall in!"

"I didn't!"

*The force field will protect you. He won't touch. He just wants
to see. Don't look up.*

I was right. I'm getting smarter than I used to be. Braver,
too: my eyes are dry. Now that the shoes are gone, I feel like
throwing up, but nothing comes. I wash my hands and face
and step into the hall, startled by Grandma Gen at the other
end, glaring. Under all that goopy black mascara, it's a miracle she can see me. But she does. "You look as if you've been
doing handstands," she says, twirling her hand, rings glinting
on every finger. "Fix your hair."

I nod, but when she walks away, I slip into the living room and curl into the tightest spot I can find, under a book-stacked coffee table. After a while, I hear voices in the kitchen.

"Mom?" It's Aunt Pat. "Can we talk for a minute?"

"Can it wait?" That's Grandma Gen.

I sit up, straining my ears.

"I was just wondering . . ." Aunt Pat speaks softly. "Did you ask Dad?"

Dishes clash under running water.

"About why he's avoiding me?" Aunt Pat adds.

"Oh. That." Grandma Gen sighs. "Yes."

"Did I do something?" Aunt Pat sounds scared. "To upset him?"

"Of course not!"

"But he hasn't said one word to me! He won't even look at—"

"Oh, do stop worrying, Patricia!"

Grandma Gen's heels click-clack on the tile floor, the sliding door rattles, and a few bars of "Blackbird" trickle over the last thing she says, which I'll never forget: "Now that you girls are grown, he feels he has to be careful. That's all."

When I'm sure it's safe, I creep into the kitchen and find Aunt Pat gripping the counter, shaking. My rock is unstable. Am I losing her? I need to bring her back. Gently, I tug her shirt. "Aunt Pat? Will you show me your altar?"

Hand in hand, we go to her room, where we're quiet for a while. She sits cross-legged on the bed, breathing in through the nose, out through the mouth, how she tells me to when

I'm jittery. On the wall above her is a poster of a woman in the same position, with glowing balls of light running up her spine. I know the balls represent the chakras, which Aunt Pat talks about a lot. Her shoulders begin to soften as I move through each item on her altar—a pink crystal, a spicy candle, a chubby stone Buddha, rosary beads like mine, from Grandma Gen's trip to Medjugorje, and a handwritten prayer on a worn scrap of paper:

> *Help us to be present to one another*
> *so that our presence may be a strength*
> *that heals the wounds of time.*

On the bookshelf, with the thick books about natural healing, organic composting, distance running, and meditation, is a section about graphic design and advertising. That's what Aunt Shawn does, draws pictures for advertisements.

"Does Aunt Shawn share your room?"

"Yes, she does."

I've never heard of grown-up friends sharing a room before, especially in such a big house. I wonder if Aunt Pat is scared of the dark, too.

On the dresser, next to a framed photo of Aunt Pat in her army nurse uniform in Vietnam, is a long piece of pinewood shellacked with pictures of a little girl and an old postcard of a hospital. Burned into the wood in slanting letters it says PATRICIA ELAINE TYLER, AUGUST 13, 1943. I pick it up, running my hand over the glossy surface.

"Grandpapa made that for me," says Aunt Pat, "for my fortieth birthday. The wood is from an old barn in Moultrie, Georgia, where I was born." She comes to my side, touches a fine crack in the wood, held together with a metal Band-Aid and two tiny screws. "See how he fixed it, so carefully?"

I twitch, pressing the thing into her hands and looking out the window. The sun is falling behind the green hills. There definitely won't be time for our hike.

"Kimberly, is anything wrong? Anything you want to talk about?"

Yes! Everything is wrong! Why are you so different today? Why does Grandpapa have to be careful? What is this shape I can't grab hold of?

"No," I say, shaking my head. We're not supposed to ask questions like that. We don't pull at threads that could unravel us.

2

WE'RE MARINES, GODDAMMIT!

"I wish you came sooner," I say to Mom.

We're on the dock, behind Dad's work yard. She stands on her tiptoes, passing the cooler up to the *Absolute*. That's the name of our boat, a Formula with a peeling yellow stripe down the side. It always breaks down, but Dad never gets tired of fixing it.

"Well, we stopped at home to pack the cooler, so you girls could stay and have fun," says Mom, "and we got you sodas!"

Fun? I want to say. *We don't have fun there.* But I can't bring myself to tell her it's not that great reliving her childhood at Earle Avenue. It would be disrespectful to say Grandma Gen hates us, and Grandpapa gives us the creeps. He isn't the same guy she talks about, who taught her how to ride a

bike and draw full moons with a compass. He's not the same
guy who fixed her toys when they broke, laying them on her
dresser for her to find when she woke up in the morning. I
don't know what happened to that guy. It's hard to believe
he ever existed, honestly. If Mom wonders what we do at her
parents', or why I only get carsick on rides there and back, she
doesn't ask. I wouldn't know how to answer, anyway. We only
left Earle Avenue an hour ago, and the weekend is already
fading like a bad dream.

I remember the grandfather clock, chiming the half hour, the
brass pendulum glinting. It was 5:30 AM. The staircase was
shades of gray. I was halfway up, shivering. My hair was sop-
ping wet, my nightgown soaked down the back. I checked
over my shoulder. No one there—just a trail of wet footprints.
Where had I been? Sleepwalking, in the rain? But the sky in
the window was starry, violet-blue, not a cloud. I opened my
mouth to call for Mom, then clamped it shut, remembering:
they were on their romantic weekend away. Collette and I
were alone with Grandpapa and Grandma Gen.

Their bedroom door was open as I passed. He wasn't there,
but she was, sitting up against her pillows in a purple ruffled
nightgown, wide awake. Our eyes met. I was dripping on her
carpet, and she didn't ask why, or even say a word. So this was
normal? Maybe it was.

I remember breakfast. Grandpapa in his royal-blue robe—
just a robe, no pajamas underneath—whistling "Ragtime" as
he sliced our toast into fingers.

Tick-tick-tick-tick-tick went the clocks.

I tried to ignore Grandpapa eating his Cream of Wheat, rolling each spoonful round and round in his mouth, as if he didn't have teeth, which he does. Pointy ones. It's important to eat slowly, he always says, for better digestion and weight maintenance.

I remember he slid a toast finger from my plate. "You don't want to eat it?" he said. "I'll have to eat it for you, then." My scalp turned freezing cold and I touched my hair, startled to find it dry.

I want to remember toppling my chair, running for the door. But I didn't do that. I didn't want to cause a scene and scare Collette, across the table in her book. Her smudgy pink glasses. Her dainty finger, twirling her hair. I could never get lost like that. Who would protect her then?

I'm starting to get warm. The sun prickles my shoulders and glows behind my closed eyes as we motor through the still marshes. Aside from the garbage smell, I love the sheltered safety of the canals. If it were up to me, we'd go no farther than the little beach behind the Oceanside sanitation department. But Dad wants Lookout Point, and our summer Sundays on the boat are the only times he doesn't have to work, so he gets his way. At the tip of Lido Beach, where the bay opens up to the ocean and the boats rock, we drop anchor. Collette jumps into the choppy water, disappearing into her too-big life vest and popping out like a turtle. I crouch on the stern, waiting for Dad to carry me on his shoulders. At the ocean, he doesn't push me to swim, or ask me what Murphys are. I don't have to swallow my fear and answer, "We're Marines, goddammit!" For once, it's enough that he's one.

Dad's greatest pride is being a Marine, but he's mysterious about the war. What stories he does tell, a few beers in, are about the exciting parts. His job, as a minesweeper, was to go ahead of his team as they searched hostile territory for explosives and land mines. How terrifying it must have been, crawling through booby traps all day long, praying on a loop not to get blown up. But Dad plays that down. It was better to be the first one into the abandoned hooch, he says. The enemy doesn't shoot the point man. They want to get everybody, so they wait. The way Dad tells it, he was the lucky one, the one with the fighting chance.

But I know it was bad. I know he slept with his gun, waiting for them to come for him. And I know he still carries that fear. I've poked him awake on the TV room floor, *Cops* blasting, and seen it up close. For the split second before he realizes I'm his daughter, Dad thinks I'm the enemy. In that split second, we're afraid, together.

For their romantic weekend, Mom got extra-long red acrylics. As she carefully peels Saran Wrap off of my bologna sandwich, her hands become Grandma Gen's hands, and I lose my appetite.

After lunch (my sandwich buried in the sand), I grab the football and follow Dad along the shore, striding long to fit my footprints inside his. There's a spot, way down past the bridge, where we can throw without bothering anybody.

"Dad," I yell into the wind, "do you miss Uncle Mike?"

"Course I do."

Uncle Mike is Dad's younger brother who died of a heroin overdose last month. He was handsome like Jesus Christ, with his bare feet and long red hair and beard. But that was where the similarities stopped. Because of the drugs, Uncle Mike wasn't allowed to come over, but Dad gave him jobs and took him to the methadone clinic every morning. Dad says Uncle Mike wanted to get better, but not badly enough.

I skip to Dad's side. "Is Uncle Mike in heaven?"

"Course he is." Dad tosses his cigarette into the blue sky. "Now, are we gonna stand around talking about this all day, or are we gonna play football?"

"Play football!" I say, the only right answer.

Since it happened, Dad is more restless than ever, like if he stops moving, he might trigger a mine and explode. I wish he would just cry. Sometimes, you have to fall apart before you can feel better. I know this from experience. Lots and lots of experience. But that's not something I share with Dad. *If it ain't broken, we don't cry* is practically our family motto. By "broken," that means on the outside, of course.

...

On Mondays, Wednesdays, and Fridays, Mom usually picks me up from school and we go to Earle Avenue, where she does Grandpapa's books and I try to stay invisible. But I haven't had to go lately. I think it's because of the Thing growing on my mouth. The fever that came with it is gone, but I'm still too ugly for Grandma Gen.

At ballet, when the teacher, says, "Smile, girls!" the Thing cracks open. I lick away the blood. You can't be invisible when your face is bleeding. I ask to be excused early and rush to the changing room to yank my snow boots over my pink tights. Mom is taking me to the doctor to get medicine.

The Thing isn't like my mosquito bite scabs. It hurts so bad that I don't even want to pick at it, which is a first. At the same time, I'm also sore where my leotard rubs against my privates. Mom says it must be a yeast infection, and I need to start changing as soon as I get home from gymnastics and ballet. She says to practice better hygiene and wear my cotton underpants, not the shiny nylon ones, and it will go away.

"I'm going to press on your neck now," says the skin doctor. His fingers are gentle, but I still flinch, crinkling the paper on the green examination chair.

"Alright now," he says, stepping back.

To Mom, he says, "It's definitely herpes."

"No!" Mom is on her feet, her tasseled leather purse plunking to the floor. "Sorry," she adds. "But she's eight. She does not have herpes."

For a long space, no one speaks. I open my jaws like a mountain lion, feeling the Thing stretch and break. *Help me.* I can't face another day like this. The doctor looks from me to Mom. "Mrs. Murphy, this a very common virus, spread easily between children in school settings."

Mom paces by the door, like she's preparing to open it and

run. "That's *not* what it is," she insists. I've never heard her be so bossy, so like Grandma Gen.

Slowly, the doctor turns to me. "Kimberly, is everything okay on your body, otherwise?"

I look at the floor, where dirty ice has dripped from my boots. I can't say out loud that my vagina is itching and burning, can I? I'm still deciding how to answer when Mom grabs my hand, pulling me to my feet.

Outside, wind whips the Thing. I gasp, licking it and jumping up and down while Mom unlocks the car. I want to ask her what's wrong with herpes and why she's so upset and why we didn't get any medicine. Isn't that what we came for? Wasn't he a doctor, after all? But the set of her mouth tells me to keep mine shut; this is just one of those times when I'll have to be confused.

We double-park outside the health food store where Aunt Pat shops when she comes to visit. Now I'm even more confused. Mom doesn't come here. It's expensive, and they don't sell vegetables in a can or Styrofoam packages of meat. It stinks of a billion vitamins mixed with stale incense and cat food. The man behind the counter looks like nobody else in Oceanside, with long hair and little round glasses, like poor John Lennon.

"We need something for this," Mom says, indicating at the Thing. "Please."

The man tilts his head, leaning over his book to peer at me. We've come to the right place, he tells us. He has a cream for herp—

"It's not herpes!" Mom repeats.

We leave, anyway, with the cream. I twist it open in the car, wave off a blast of garlic and licorice, and dab some on the Thing as I say a silent prayer for good measure: *Please heal me, Virgin Mary.*

But the Thing gets worse and worse, spreading up my cheek to form a half-Joker smile that I take to hiding with my hand at school, all the while seething at Mary, who never, ever listens to me. After a couple weeks, the Thing gets tired and shrinks back to the size of a tadpole, then a pea, then a few flecks of sand. Finally, it retreats back to where it came from—inside me, I assume—and I'm pretty enough to go to Earle Avenue again.

On visiting days, I actually wish the Thing would come back. I even consider the possibility that Mary *was* listening, and didn't heal me on purpose, to protect me. To be a monster, marked on the outside for all to see, is one way to be safe.

3

A.D.

1987

Ten years old

Mom is two minutes late for pickup. She is never, ever late. Spotting her car, I peel away from my wall and break into a careful, shuffling run across the yard. Pigeons diving for potato chip bags; rowdy kids, shoving and yelling. At school, everything is a threat. Every day unfolds in slow motion, like one long horror movie. I can't wait to be safe in the front seat, though I won't get to loosen my belt and untie my shoelaces and properly breathe for at least a couple more hours, when we're home from Earle Avenue.

Only it isn't our wagon at the curb, but Uncle Chap and Aunt Helen's identical one. Locking my door, I turn to search Aunt Helen's plainly pretty face. Aunt Helen is Mom's best friend. They're so much alike, people think they're sisters by blood, but they're the kind who are married to brothers. Like

Mom, Aunt Helen only wears makeup on special occasions, but keeps her nails Grandma Gen–level done. Like Mom, she uses them to tickle and gently scratch, never to jab and punish. I chose her to be my confirmation sponsor, and when I need to be strong, I say my confirmation name quietly to myself: *"Kimberly Shannon Helen Murphy."*

"Your mom's fine!" Aunt Helen reassures me, pulling away from the zoo. "But your Grandpapa had a fall and hit his head on the kitchen counter. He's in the hospital to get checked out." Aunt Helen reaches across the seat to rake my ponytail, glancing between the road and me. "Don't you worry, Kimberly Shannon. He's going to be okay."

I nod, relaxing into my seat. I'm not worried.

At bedtime, as I hold my iron cross and say my prayers, I don't ask for Grandpapa to get better. I know it's a sin of omission, but that's fine; I'll take hell if I have to.

The second night, I wake to find Mom at the foot of my bed, her shoulders shaking. She doesn't have to tell me he's dead. Hanging my head for cover, I reach down inside myself, feeling around for sadness. It isn't there. All I feel is calm.

...

Many years later, Dad will relish the story. In his telling, they kept Grandpapa overnight for observation. Sometime the next afternoon, when Grandma Gen left his side to change her clothes and put her lips back on, he was sitting up in bed, hooked to beeping machines and eating green Jell-O. I imagine he was whistling between bites—drawing out his pleasure—though Dad doesn't say that. Dad says: "When your mom walked in his room, Grandpapa took one look at her, died on the spot!"

Then came the terrible noise, the dying-animal scream, ringing through the room, down the hallways, out the open windows. Mom covered her ears, not realizing it was coming from her.

Finally, Dad will add the kicker: "Perfect justice," he'll say, shaking his head. "It was perfect justice." Hardly.

But Dad's story isn't true, anyway. He wasn't even there. Mom, who went to the hospital alone, says Grandpapa was already dead when she walked in. She did make the terrible dying-animal sound. She says it was a howl of sorrow, but maybe it was something else. I think it was her trapped self being released—only to turn around and crawl back inside. Mom wasn't ready for the knowledge it held.

...

The funeral is at St. Agnes in Rockville Centre, where Grandma Gen married Grandpapa and Mom married Dad. In the vestibule, Mom puts her fingers in the holy water and makes the sign of the cross. When she's not looking, I sidle past the bowl, spared from touching the same water all those germy fingers before us have touched. If they make us take

communion today, I'll put out my hand (never my tongue) for
the stale cracker, but I'll only pretend to put it in my mouth.
Eating the broken body of Jesus is *just what we do*, Mom always says, which isn't a reason at all.

Wedged between Mom and Collette in the second pew,
I'm thin as a sliver, my stomach rumbling through my black
velvet dress. I've hardly eaten the whole week since he died.
At first, I wasn't hungry. Now I'm starving, and it feels good.
My body is mine to feed or not feed, to do with what I want.
I don't know why this never occurred to me before.

The organ music reminds me of Grandpapa's player piano,
but it would be rude to cover my ears. In the gaps between
notes of "Amazing Grace," the nave echoes with sniffles and
coughs and my cousin Amanda's whimpering. The coffin—
closed, thankfully—is decorated with a blanket of roses and
a bright red sash with Grandma Gen's and his saying, I Got
You, Babe, in glitter.

Grandma Gen must have bought every last white rose in
the state of New York: garlands wind around candlesticks and
line the pews; wreaths tilt on Eiffel Tower stands; arrange-
ments explode from vases as tall as me. When I put my nose
in one, it has no scent.

She sits with my aunts in the first row, silty rivers running
down her cheeks and one eye that looks to be bleeding; she
dabs it with Grandpapa's blue silk handkerchief, obviously
embarrassed. Her face is her pride and joy.

"What happened to Grandma Gen?" I whisper to Collette.

My sister looks up from the open Bible on her lap. "Burst
blood vessel," she whispers, "from crying." My sister's eyes are

as dry as mine. I wonder if she's being a Marine, but I suspect not. I suspect she reached down for her sadness and came up empty-handed, like me. Something is obviously wrong with us, but I've always known that.

At the top of the marble steps, they rest his box—red mahogany, like the inside of Earle Avenue—on a carved stone table. As the priest moves around it, sprinkling holy water, I wonder what Grandpapa's wearing in there. His pin-striped suit, probably, with a rosebud in the buttonhole. His shiny tasseled shoes, I hope.

"Death is not the end," the priest tells us, "nor does it break the bonds forged in life. . . ."

That can't be true, can it? I rip a cuticle with my teeth. Mom pulls my hand away from my mouth and covers it with hers as, one by one, my aunts and uncles walk to the pulpit to talk about a kind, generous man I've never met.

Aunt Pat wants Grandpapa to watch over us. "Please help us with your guiding hands," she asks him in his coffin.

Please don't.

Aunt Daphne tells us, in her whispery Marilyn Monroe voice: "Dad reminded me of Jesus—humble, kind, and giving."

"He was a man of amazing self-control," says Uncle Jon.

Maybe they're talking about Grandpapa's Gemini twin. That was his sign, which I know because Aunt Pat gave him a horoscope birthday card one year. The illustration was a man with one body and two heads. It was a good card for Grandpapa.

Uncle Chris, as always, has the longest speech. "I was four or five," he reads stiffly from his notes, "and Dad was working on an elaborate set of floor plans for a new building. I jumped upon his lap, knocking over a bottle of ink, which ran down the drawing table, all over the work he had just finished." Polite laughter ripples through the pews, and Uncle Chris shakes his head, continuing: "Most fathers would have flown into a rage, but Dad just quietly put me down, picked up some tissue paper, and started blotting up the black pools of ink. . . ."

I can barely hear him by "ink." Miraculously, I've floated out of my body, all the way up to the eaves, above the organist and Jesus on his cross. Up here in the stained glass light, all I can hear is my own heart.

Down there, my empty, small body slumps when Mom stands up, smoothing her skirt. She's going to tell more lies about him, but I don't have to listen. Nothing can reach me up here. It's incredible! Where did I learn to float like this—in the bathroom?

Grandpapa, do you remember?

He doesn't answer, of course. Now he'll never have to.

...

After the funeral, I'll never say "Grandpapa" again. He doesn't have to be "my grandfather" anymore, either. If I have to talk about him, I'll say, "Mom's father," "Grandma Gen's husband," "Edward," or better, just plain old "him."

4

ROBBED

1987
Still ten

A few days after the funeral, Grandma Gen went to the salon and returned to find her bedroom window open, her jewelry (except the usual ton she puts on to leave the house) missing. Now, Mom says Grandma Gen is afraid to be alone, and *I* have to stay with her, *all summer long.*

"What am I supposed to do if the robber comes back?" I protest. "Stab him with a kitchen knife?"

"Grandma Gen doesn't need a bodyguard," Mom says. "She just needs your company."

That's the end of the conversation, and my summer plans. No gymnastics camp, no ballet. Nothing to take me away from Grandma Gen's side.

———

I do leave her side, every chance I get. When we're not at the beach, working on our tans, or at St. Agnes, lighting candles for him, I tiptoe around the house—everywhere but the basement—playing silently by myself. The trick is to be out of sight, but close enough that I can hear her calling when she "needs" me. I can spend hours circling Grandma Gen, trying not to explode. Every few rounds, I dart into the bathroom to sneak a puff on my new inhaler. It feels like magic going in, like nothing can hurt me.

I got the medicine on my first day back to school after he died. The morning started off alright. I was running after a ball, tilting my face to the sun, happy not to be cooped up with my crying family anymore. Then came the shadow on my shoulders, the whiff of Old Spice and stale breath. I spun around. The shadow followed. Like a snake, it slid inside me, coiling around my lungs, taking my breath. I backed into the playground fence, wrapped my fingers around the chain links, and blacked out.

Mom came and drove me straight to the pediatrician, who stabbed me with an adrenaline shot, and another. When the squeezing let go, the doctor said, "That must have been scary, huh?" I nodded. *Yeah, it was scary!* It was a ghost. It was *him.* How did the doctor know? It turned out he didn't; he just thought I had asthma. If the medicine for that was anything like the stuff in the shot, I wanted it.

Mom just kept shaking her head. "She's never had that before. Why would she have it now?" But asthma must be a

better disease to have than herpes because she accepted the doctor's prescription.

At night, Grandma Gen and I watch *Perry Mason* and *I Love Lucy*. I sit next to her on the sofa, on the opposite side of her popped eye. She doesn't like anyone seeing it, and that's fine with me. Grandma Gen tucks her feet under her, but I sit at attention, scanning the room for ghosts. I'm allowed to eat two pretzels for dessert.

When Grandma Gen picks up her I LOVE MY HUSBAND mug and pulls the chain on the Tiffany light, she's ready for bed. This is the worst part of the day, the part I've been waiting to get over with since I opened my eyes this morning. Sneaking off my socks, I follow her, sideways, up the gleaming stairs. The clock on the landing is silent now. She doesn't know how to wind it, and I'll never tell her that he showed me. At the top, where their wedding portrait hangs, she pauses for her nightly ritual. I wait with my back to the wall while she kisses her fingertips, touches them to his lips. "I got you, Babe," she says.

There are three other bedrooms in the house, but I have to sleep with her, on his side. I lie straight as a nail while Grandma Gen clicks her rosary and whispers one Hail Mary for each bead on the string. All fifty-nine of them.

"Hail Mary, full of grace.

The Lord is with thee.

Blessed art thou amongst women,

and blessed is the fruit of thy womb, Jesus.

Holy Mary, Mother of God,
pray for us sinners,
now and at the hour of our death.
Amen."

We fall asleep to the AM Catholic station, the archbishop's sermon crackling through the darkness. He talks about obeying God, handing our hearts to God. "God looks after those who trust in him completely," he says, explaining a lot about my life.

"Kimberly, wake up."

I gasp awake. The red letters on the digital clock say 5:00, the same time he always comes.

...

Hewlett Point is no Rockville Links—the pool is cloudy, the beach is small and crowded, and there are lockers instead of cabanas—but Grandma Gen likes to swim in the bay, and this is where they met when they were teenagers. Even though he preferred the country club, Hewlett's *their* place. We go every weekday, meeting Mom and Collette on good days. Today, we pick up Grandma Gen's only friend, Shirley. She's barely fastened her seat belt when the stories begin.

"My first impression of Ed was *what a show-off*!" says Grandma Gen, rolling through a stop sign. "He was so strong and wiry, doing gymnastics and diving and drawing palm trees on girls' legs! Thank goodness, I was very athletic. I was the only girl who could outrun him."

"Ha!" pipes Shirley, picking her ashy teeth in the visor mirror.

I'm in the back, next to my boom box, which hogs three-quarters of the seat. In my skirt pocket, I pop my blisters— *one, two, three, four*—with my thumbnail. This morning, passing through the kitchen, I nervously bounced my fingers along the electric stovetop. It turned out to be on. I didn't scream as I smelled my flesh burning. *Good girl*, said his voice in my head. *You know how carelessness upsets her.*

Down the beach, I spot Mom and Aunt Helen, facing the bay. Collette is wrapped in a towel, nose in a book.

"Mom!" I wave, breaking into a run. I want to tell her about the burn before Grandma does. I want to tell it my way, before she tells it hers—I'm always bad in Grandma Gen's stories. But she catches up, bracelets clinking under her caftan.

"*Helloooo*, baby dolls!" she trills, grabbing my hand and holding it to Mom's face. "Kathy, do you see what Kimberly did? I turned my back for one minute, and she tried to hide it from me!"

"It hurts," I say, pulling my hand back. "Maybe I should see a doctor?"

Mom doesn't think so. She usually seems calm after an accident, even relieved; the crisis is over and no matter how bad it was, odds are there won't be another one right away.

———

At the lockers, she unpeels the paper towels from my hand; it stinks of milk of magnesia, my grandparents' nonremedy for everything. "You must tell Grandma Gen if you're hurt," says Mom. "Why didn't you tell her?"

I bite my cheek.

"Because she scares me." There. My body relaxes. If the truth feels so good, why don't we say it more?

I look at Mom, and there's my answer, in her darkening eyes, her downturned mouth. "Why would you say that, Kimberly?" She shuts the first aid kit. "Your grandmother loves you!"

The truth always hurts Mom. The truth isn't worth it. It's easier to say sorry, so I do. When she's finished cleaning me up, I give Mom my good hand, let her lead me back.

Grandma Gen and Shirley are settled in their folding chairs, bathing suit straps down on their wrinkly shoulders. "I miss him most at dinnertime," says Grandma Gen to nobody and everybody. "He used to—"

"Would you, Kimberly?" Shirley points to her umbrella, lying folded at her feet.

"Um . . ." I look at my fresh bandages, already oozing. I shrug. "Sure."

With my good hand, I try jamming the blunt pole into the sand, but it just falls over, so I dig a hole, then march to the water with Collette's plastic pail for some wet sand. After several trips, I raise my umbrella-spear overhead.

"Raaahhhhh!" I yell, thrusting it deep. "There you go, Shirley!"

Grabbing my boom box, I march across the sand and out of their sight.

On the splintery picnic deck, where nobody goes, I set the stereo down. I press Play. "There comes a time," sings Lionel Richie, "when we heed a certain call."

I take my position, raising my arms to begin the routine I should be perfecting at gymnastics camp this summer. It's going to hurt, but let it. I dive forward into a handstand split. Holding for a moment, I continue into a crooked front walkover, a wobbly lunge, a sorry excuse for a back walkover.

Gymnastics is supposed to be the place where my body never betrays me, where it does what I want it to, no matter what hurts. But my body has grown nearly two inches in two months, and it won't be contained. I can't make it override the pain in my fingers or the rage that bubbles up when I think of my lost summer. Again and again, I push through my routine. Again and again, I blow it.

I press Stop on the boom box. Nothing it plays sounds any good. It was a communion gift. Not even a year ago, Mom's father brought it to my party in our backyard. Everyone came, both sides of the family. Dad lit the grill while I stood for more pictures in my white dress with the veil that fell to my shoulders. I wanted to change, but my aunts and uncles kept saying, "One more!" so I kept still and smiling like my communion doll.

The stereo was stuck with a silver bow. I took it, thanking him. There was a tape inside the deck. I punched the button and removed it: "We Are the World," just that one song, was on both sides. I pretended to read every tiny word on the plastic. Even when we weren't alone, it felt like we were.

"Well?" he said. "Aren't you going to play it?"

"Maybe later," I said.

"Go on," he teased. "What are you so afraid of?"

There it was, the dare, the bait. Hating us both, I played the song.

Now, collapsed on the deck, heaving and dripping with sweat, it strikes me that I don't hate myself so much anymore. When he died, something broke open in me. A small glimmer of strength flickered up through the crack. I don't know where it came from, but I think it's keeping me alive.

5

REMEMBERING

1991

Fourteen-going-on-fifteen years old

"Angel of God, my guardian dear,
   to whom God's love commits me here.
   Ever this day be at my side,
   to light and guard,
   to rule and guide.
   Amen."

"Amen," repeats Mom, squeezing me a notch tighter before releasing me.

I'm a freshman, and we still say the Angel of God prayer every morning before I walk out the door. Mom still reminds me to look both ways before I cross the street to Oceanside High, which is massive and takes up the entire opposite side of the block. When school's in session, Skillman Avenue is busy, but the speed limit is twenty-five, so it's not as if I have to cross the Long Island Expressway. But, as Mom reminds me every morning, "Teenage drivers are naturally distracted."

"Don't worry," I tell her, lugging my letterman's jacket over my shoulders. "I promise to be careful."

And I will. I'm still a good girl, mostly. My priorities are still simple and automatic: stay alive, excel at cheerleading, dance, and gymnastics, and try to ease Mom's worries. She's been extra anxious and distracted lately. I'll come home to find her pacing back and forth in the kitchen, talking to Aunt Pat or Aunt Kristy on the phone, the coiled cord stretching, sagging, stretching, each time she crosses the room. She doesn't say why she's acting strange, and I don't have time to wonder. I've been so busy with school activities and hanging out with my best friends, Mary and Michele. The rare times that I'm home before dinner, Mom is often out, which is weird, because my whole life, home is where she's been, at least physically. We don't know where she goes. When I ask, she says, "I don't need to tell you girls where I am every second."

Stepping into the frosty air in my too-short cheerleading skirt, I twirl to wave at Mom in the door in her bathrobe. Her cheeks are flushed, her expression full of pride. It fills *me* with pride that I'm in the small category of people and things that give her strength. For Mom, the fact that I'm a cheerleader means I'm happy and popular, and cancels out the fact that my skirt hardly covers my briefs. It did a month ago, but my legs keep growing, so much that my gymnastics coach is talking about dropping me, but my dance teachers are happy. Anyway, for me, being a cheerleader isn't a ticket to happiness, just the closest I can come to being a Marine without enlisting. It gives me an identity to hide behind. I don't have to seal my body up in double undershirts and too-tight belts anymore. My cheerleading uniform is my armor; I just wish there was more of it.

I can point to the date I stopped wanting to be invisible so badly: it was the summer after I stayed with Grandma Gen at Earle Avenue. We had a big family reunion on a lake in Virginia with all my aunts and uncles and cousins. I spent my days rolling down hills, playing Slip 'n Slide, and lounging on my inner tube on the dark lake. One afternoon as I waded to the shore, shimmering wet, Mom called from the picnic table, "Kimberly, why don't you show us your gymnastics routine?"

Instead of wanting to wither up and die, I performed the three-minute routine right on the spot in front of everyone, even Grandma Gen. Everyone but her seemed so happy that summer. Aunt Pat was back to being her old self, only more relaxed than I'd ever seen her. Unlike the rest of us, she didn't worry about the moccasin snakes that slithered across the lake's surface. She'd jump off the dock, peel off her bathing suit underwater, toss it onto the dock, and swim into the distance. Hours later, she'd return to the dock, slip her suit back on, and emerge with a blissful expression. Together, we'd lie on the grass, wrapped in our beach towels, until the sun began to fall and goose bumps covered our tanned arms.

Now, a cluster of senior guys stare as I walk across the green, but I smile right past them, waving at Mary and Michele, also in Oceanside High Sailors cheer uniforms, their ponytails—

Mary's strawberry-blond and Michele's buttercup-yellow like mine—in white scrunchies, too. I hold my chin up and skip the last steps through crackling maple leaves toward my friends, my saviors. Mary and Michele are always laughing—and me, too, when I'm with them. I hug them as if I don't feel those guys' eyes on my exposed thighs, making the skin burn and prickle. Importantly, I don't tug down my skirt; I won't give them that satisfaction.

I've been a cheerleader since seventh grade. That's how I met Mary and Michele. The two of them have been friends since birth; their moms met at the hospital where they were born. Like me, Mary was born on December 16, 1976. Michele was born on December 17. The stars were apparently out of whack in that twenty-four-hour period, or maybe it's just a coincidence that none of us has had it so easy in life. Michele's mom has been diagnosed with a brain tumor. Mary's dad died when she was little, and her mom, Toni, has struggled ever since, leaving Mary to be the grown-up in the house. I haven't lived through a single tragedy that I know of, but I feel as if I have, so we understand each other. After cheerleading, we usually go to Mary's house, because Toni lets us do whatever we want. We turn up the music and sing at the top of our lungs into our hairbrushes or raid Toni's closet and take modeling pictures with our Le Clic cameras.

It's not lost on me that this confident girl who flips her hair and flirts with boys and cheers on the varsity squad only fully awoke in my body after Grandma Gen sold Earle Avenue and moved to Marin. That was a year ago, and ever since—with no one *tsk*-ing over my shoulder—I've been coloring myself in, faster and faster.

I'm onto something, but only the tip of it.

One night, Mom and I are watching TV. She's wrapped in the fuzzy tiger-print blanket we've had my whole life, and I'm curled at her feet on the floor, wearing sweatpants and two sweatshirts. Both Mom and I are always cold. And we both love Lifetime movies. Right now, we're being sucked into the beginning of one about a family that looks perfect on the outside but is most likely rotten on the inside—the usual Lifetime fare.

Everything is in soft focus. The main character has stiff blond hair, frosted pink lips, and diamond-post earrings, just like in the Zales commercials they show during the breaks. The woman is about thirty, visiting her father's house. In his study, she picks up a music box—a tiny ballerina, captive in a glass dome. She turns a key on the bottom, and a mechanical tune begins to play. Watching the dancer's slow pirouette, the woman disappears from herself. The show cuts to black-and-white—a stuffed horse, bobbing in a man's hand. The woman starts to shake and sweat, struggling for breath. Her eyes fly open as a door in my head does the same: *That's how I feel!*

Now the character remembers: her father abused her. "It's been a week since I've known," she sobs into her husband's arms, "and I still answer Dad's phone calls. I still want to impress him."

"How can you be sure it happened?" asks the husband. "That you're not imagining it?"

"I just *know*," she says.

My thoughts are shuffling all around, trying to make sense of how the story on TV might match up with mine. But I have no story.

All I know is I've been seeing things—flashes of scary movies that I've never watched before—movies about me.

Once, I saw my hands, wadding a pair of bloody underwear in toilet paper, burying it deep in the bathroom garbage. Another time, I saw myself waking in a strange bed, naked on the bottom, when I *always* sleep in pajamas. And just the other day, I thought I saw a man in the corner of my room. I dove into my closet, rocking myself till the nightmare faded away.

But what if it wasn't a nightmare? What if it was a memory?

"Mom, I think something like that happened to me!"

As soon as the words leave my lips, a voice inside me demands, *Why are you lying?*

Am I lying? How could anything so terrifying *not* be real?

Mom stares at the screen, her expression stuck.

I shake her arm. "Mom?"

Flipping back the blanket, she stands up, veering drunkenly from the room. But Mom's not drunk, she only drinks at family parties.

Soon she's back, not wobbly anymore. "You're not going to school tomorrow," she announces, turning off the TV. "I'm taking you to talk to my therapist."

I almost laugh. "*You* have a therapist?" It's impossible.

Mom isn't like that. In our family, we don't talk to therapists, we crack jokes about therapists. Or the kind of people who go to them, that is: Manhattan people. *People who take themselves too serious*, Dad would say.

"Never mind about me," says Mom, karate-chopping a throw pillow. "Time for bed!"

"But why do you have a therapist?" I tug the sleeve of her robe, trying to pull her back to the couch, but she won't budge.

"Because someone hurt me, too," she answers.

Did she actually say that, and now she's leaving? I follow her into her dark room, where Dad is sleeping because the TV room was taken. He has to get up super early for work, so I have to be quiet. "*Who hurt you?*" I whisper. She burrows under the covers, turning her back to me. "*Mom?*" I kneel by the bed, shake her hip. "*Do you know who it was?*"

"*Yes*," she whispers.

And with that, a realization: it was my Snoopy underwear, with the bloodstains! I wore them only once, to the Christmas party, the year I got them in my stocking. I see myself afterward—throwing them away, then wrapping myself in a towel and squishing into the little space next to the toilet. I see myself banging my head on the wall, not too hard, just hard enough. I used to do that, after Earle Avenue, didn't I?

"*Was it your father?*" I whisper.

Mom's breathing gets faster and faster. She flips over to face me. Pulling me in, she whispers into my hair: "*I didn't remember till this year. I locked it up behind my steel door, and I forgot. I swear I forgot.*"

I pull away. "What steel door?"

But she doesn't seem to hear me, just keeps whispering, over and over, that she forgot.

...

"Come in, both of you." The therapist waves Mom and me into a small office crammed with worn furniture and latch-hook rugs. The basement room is below a peeling white clapboard house, a lot like ours, but closer to the droning LIE. The only window is a mud-splattered rectangle hovering above the therapist's cluttered desk. A lump of crabgrass, a sliver of cold sky.

Is this where you've been disappearing to all these months? I want to ask Mom. *You come here voluntarily?* She drops into a threadbare armchair in the corner, leaving me to take the one facing the therapist's desk.

The therapist wears all-brown clothes, blending with the furniture. She's trying to camouflage herself, so I forget she's here and act natural. It won't work. There's nothing natural about this. I should be at school.

Flipping open a skinny spiral notebook, like detectives use on Dad's murder shows, she tips back and looks me up and down, searching for clues.

"So, Kimberly," the therapist says, "your mom tells me you've been having some pretty upsetting memories?"

I look at Mom for help. Are we even sure they're memories? But Mom's somewhere else, sliding her cross back and forth on its chain as she chews her bottom lip—a habit we both have. *You're just like your mother*, he used to say.

"I think so?" I hear myself answer.

"Good, good," says the therapist, scribbling on her note-pad. "Can you describe these flashbacks?"

Good? I want to say. *Flashbacks?* Is that what they're called? The word fits how it feels.

I drum my chair leg with my foot. Mom is so checked out, I can forget about my manners.

"Close your eyes, if it helps," the therapist prompts.

"No, thank you." I don't want to revisit those awful flash-backs, and I definitely don't want to tell *her* about them. I just want Mom to explain what's happening. She knows, and she won't tell me! *Was it your father?* I asked. She didn't get mad at me for suggesting such a thing. She didn't even say a simple no.

"What are you thinking right now?" The therapist hovers her pen over the notebook.

I shake my head. "Nothing." What's in my head is none of her business. None of this is any of her business. It's our business, Mom's and mine.

"Kim, please!" Mom's back, digging her nails into the arms of her chair like a very tense cat. "Just tell her what you re-membered, honey," she pleads.

I pull my knees to my chest, hiding my face. "I think I was"—I search for the word the lady on the TV show used— "abused?"

The therapist scratches some notes. "By whom?"

A tall man in dim yellow light, the rectangle of a door—I shake my head.

"Kimberly," the therapist pushes. "Who hurt you?"

The shadow man appears, standing over me. I jerk to my feet, frantically searching the room, but it's just Mom and the therapist lady, staring. So I'm crazy. That's why I'm here. I shake out my hands and pull back my hair. The therapist pushes a tissue box across her desk, and I notice I'm sobbing. It's starting to hit me: everything's different now. I'm not the same person I was yesterday. I'm not that Kimberly who set the dinner table in my new toe shoes last night, dropping each paper napkin with an arabesque. That was before the Lifetime movie, when my number one priority was to break in those stiff shoes before class this weekend. Is that what I cared about, just twelve hours ago?

"Take a minute," says the therapist, who seems small and far away now. "Then let's try again."

I look out her ugly little window at her ugly weeds, grinding my teeth.

"This is a safe space," the lady says, as if just saying it makes it true. "You can tell me whatever's on your mind."

"Fine," I say, back on my feet. "I want to go home."

...

Some days pass, one or two, it doesn't matter. Life doesn't feel real in this limbo between my old world and the new one I'm falling into. One evening, I come home from gymnastics to hear Mom and Dad fighting in their room. Running upstairs to pull Collette's door closed, I find my sister on her bed, reading; she doesn't even look up. Since my memories came out and everything got so tense around here, my sister's magical ability to vanish into her books and schoolwork seems to have grown more powerful than it already was. I wonder where she is in her imagination right now. It must be better than here. Dad hasn't been home for dinner since I told Mom about my flashbacks, and she's been disappearing more and more for the "me time" that I now know is spent in group meetings with other "survivors" and in that dank therapy basement.

My parents' voices are getting louder behind their closed door. "I believe her, Bill!" Mom shouts.

"There's *no* way!" booms Dad. I picture him shaking his head, reaching for his cigarettes, which he's not allowed to smoke in their room anymore.

Mom fiercely blows her nose. She's probably sitting on the edge of their bed, looking out the bay windows her father put in, at our decrepit swing set. It's a windy night, and I can hear the swing chains clanking against the metal frame from out here in the hallway.

"I'm telling you," Mom insists, "Dad did it to her, too!"

"Nope!" says Dad. "Not on my watch. Nope. Nope."

I hear a muffled, "*Grrrrr!*" Mom screaming into a pillow? I feel the same way. Why won't he listen? Why won't he believe me?

"Come on, Kath." I imagine Dad giving Mom his cross-armed, Marine sergeant look. "You know what a drama queen she is. She probably found that goddamn book of yours, and now she thinks she was abused, too!"

"She's never even seen that book!" snaps Mom, not backing

down. "But if she did, so what? I read it. Do you think I made everything up, too?"

"Of course not," says Dad, a little softer now. He believes her, at least? "But kids make stuff up. Remember that story on the news? That preschool in California where the kids accused their teachers of satanic rituals or some baloney? People's lives were destroyed, and it never happened, is all I'm saying."

I vanish into my room as Dad steps into the hallway. Minutes later, he's banging out "Goodnight Saigon" on his drums in the basement. Dishes clatter in the kitchen. I creep into their bedroom, which is all tidied up, any signs that our world has been turned upside down erased. The worn thrift-store secretary is spotless, the pillows are plumped, and the bedspread on Great-Grandma's heavy rosewood bed is smooth. It's as businesslike and impersonal as a motel room.

All Mom and Dad have for decoration is their eleven-by-sixteen framed wedding portrait on top of the armoire. I take it down and study them—Mom in fitted cream satin, Dad in a white tuxedo jacket, black bow tie and white corsage, his hands wrapping nearly around her tiny waist. They're standing in profile, in front of a white-curtained window, almost silhouettes. Mom's hair, worn loose under her trailing veil, wasn't short and silvery yet, but long and chestnut brown. She was only twenty-one when they got married. I can't imagine the pressure she felt to be the perfect bride.

Dad looks at his perfect bride with adoration; she looks back with . . . nothing. It's that look I've known my whole life: You could snap your fingers in front of her face, and she wouldn't even blink. I always thought she was tired from taking care of us—dead tired from all the shopping and driving and cooking and mending and cleaning and organizing and keeping us looking nice and polished. It never occurred to me that she was this way even before us.

Quietly, I replace the portrait, looking around for the book Dad was talking about, the one he thinks gave me "ideas." But the only object on Mom's nightstand is her latest Harlequin romance from the library, so I push aside the mirrored accordion doors to her closet, clicking the chain on the bare lightbulb. It's pretty barren in there—a couple pairs of pressed slacks hanging on plastic hangers, her satin party blouses in a dry-cleaning bag, and some shoeboxes on the floor. On top of one is a thick library book in a clear plastic jacket, titled *The Courage to Heal: A Guide for Women Survivors of Childhood Sexual Abuse.*

I stare at that purple lettering for a long time, trying to wrap my brain around its mystery. I have a fuzzy idea what *childhood sexual abuse* is. How could I forget it happening to *me*? Maybe Dad's right and I did read this book; I just forgot I did. Maybe the words slipped through the holey pockets of my memory as so many things seem to, but the ideas stuck. His theory isn't crazy. I've been known to go through Mom's *Encyclopedia of Common Diseases* and diagnose myself with all sorts of ailments. Last month, I was sure I had a brain tumor. I'm still not convinced I don't.

Not on my watch, Dad said. Of course he wouldn't let someone hurt me. Dad has a reputation for being a good man, but people take one look at his catcher's mitt hands and mind their business. They're a little bit scared of Dad. But only people who don't know him, I remember, picturing Mom's father and Dad drinking and laughing by the fireplace at Earle Avenue. I pick up the book, open to a random page: "Many survivors feel different from other people . . . that there's something wrong deep down inside." Softly, I close the cover, the words *sexual* and *abuse* clicking together like the reassuring latch of an airplane seat belt.

...

Mom and I have a new bedtime ritual. After I've said my prayers and gotten into bed, she comes to kiss my forehead, then sits on the corner by my feet and says, "Do you want to talk?"

Always, desperately. I have so many questions: How is it possible that she didn't remember anything until last year, when she was thirty-eight, and I'm remembering now? *What* does she remember? If she would just tell me, it might help me understand my flashbacks, which have been getting scarier, even though they're still all jumbly—like I'm being sucked into an old broken TV that flips between channels and fuzzes out in the important parts. If only I had my whole life on VHS so I could rewind and see it all, just to understand.

All I've figured out for sure is it was Mom's father, and it happened more than once. *Why didn't you notice?* That's the question I want to ask most of all. *Why didn't you stop it?*

But each night, as Mom sits and waits, I'm silent. I close my eyes and grip my iron cross under my pillow.

I think I act like this because I'm still mad about being lobbed off to her therapist. Even though that's over now. The last few times I went, I refused to say a single word, so Mom stopped taking me. Also, I'm sick and tired of everything being on everyone else's terms.

After Mom leaves, I lie there for an hour or so, then tiptoe into her room and whisper into the darkness: "I'm ready to talk now."

Mom doesn't usually respond. Maybe I don't want her to, after all. Some nights I just turn and leave. Others, I gently shake her ankle under the covers until she groans and mutters, "We'll talk tomorrow, Kim." But we never do.

Mary and Michele will listen. But how could they possibly understand what I'm going through when I don't even get it myself? Instead of talking about what happened to me, or Michele's mom's brain tumor, or Mary's loneliness, we spend most of our time inventing boy dramas and chugging boxed wine and holding each other's hair over the toilet. I'm starting to get why my family likes drinking so much.

I find other ways of coping. I've figured out how to make myself throw up. On bad nights, I go to the kitchen and stuff my face with whatever I can get my hands on. Then I go to the bathroom and stick my fingers down my throat. Have a memory, throw up. Have another memory, throw up. I don't think of it as bulimia, because it's not about purging calories, it's about purging him. How good it feels to get him out. How clean I feel afterward. Each time is a new beginning.

One winter evening, when Collette is at a sleepover and Mom and Dad are on a rare date night at MacArthur Park Bar, I perform this ritual, then discover a new one. Mom's dual-blade Gillette razor is sitting on the tub's edge. I use it to slice my forehead—just above my right eyebrow. *Where she'll have to see it.* Two blades, two slices. It doesn't hurt, but it bleeds some. I lean into the mirror, waiting for the fine red lines to swell up and run over, but the cuts stay on the surface like pen marks. I smudge them with my thumb, wincing. It's still not enough.

I get the ketchup bottle from the kitchen and return to the bathroom. I unscrew the cap and dip my pinky finger into the mouth and smear the red liquid across my cuts. It stings; my mascara runs. Better. Next, I swallow a few Tylenol tablets, chasing them with some NyQuil. The sickly sweet syrup melts my limbs, smooths my brain, floats me into the hallway. At the top of the stairs, I collapse and push myself, headfirst, *b-b-bumping d-d-downward,* until I land at the bottom, rug-burned ribs and sticky face pressed into the shag carpet. My shirt is tangled up around my armpits, exposing my bra, but I don't fix it. I drift, waiting for Mom and Dad to come home and find me.

Because what I need now is for Mom, whose greatest fear in life is that her girls will suffer some freakish accident and never be perfect again, to get it: her greatest fear has arrived.

Kimberly! I imagine she'll cry, taking me in her arms. *You could have died!*

I know, I'll say. *Now will you take me to a hospital?* I've been begging them for weeks to take me somewhere safe, where I can't hurt myself, and I'll get well enough that I won't want to anymore. The answer has been no. No daughter of Dad's is going to any funny farm. We'll see, after tonight.

At last, a burst of cold air from the front hall, the stomp of snow boots on the mat, the rustle of coats. Still "passed out," I turn my face so they can see it. I can smell the bar on them as they approach and stoop over my body, inspecting me.

But there's no horrified gasp, no sobbing embrace. Mom just sighs. Her footsteps back away. Can she just leave me here, like roadkill? But I'm still half alive!

I hear her in the kitchen, now. Water splashes into the teakettle, a chair scrapes.

"Oh, for chrissakes, Kim," says Dad. I feel him stepping over me, heading upstairs. "Just get up."

PART II

SPINNING

6

GIMME SHELTER

2000

Twenty-three years old

The elevator is broken again, so I take the stairs to the fifth floor—sideways, looking over my shoulder. "Pure" by Blue Six throbs through the crumbling Bedford-Stuyvesant building— "Feel alive, feel alive, look at me, I'm free." I know exactly where it's coming from.

Safely in my apartment, I throw the locks, tear off my layers, and join my roommates, Serge and Natasha, on the living room dance floor. The futon where I sleep is shoved against the banging radiator, and every window is wide open to the freezing winter air, but the place still reeks of prehistoric cat pee and BO and Chinese takeout.

This is my new life. Natasha and I met two years ago in Marin, where Mom moved us after she and Dad got divorced and I graduated high school. I enrolled as a dance major at the College of Marin, and Natasha was in my program. After graduation, we came to New York City together to find work as dancers, which sort of panned out. We got jobs at a Long Island party production company called EJM that provides dancers for bar mitzvahs. For three hundred fifty dollars plus tips per party, we pass out glow sticks, get the kids riled up, and teach them dance moves. That's how we met EJM's star emcee, Serge, who invited us to be his roommates. The place is fine. We hear gunshots some nights, but the corner drug dealer, G-Money, looks out for me when I power walk from the subway after dark; and Serge and his uncle, the building manager, are like big brothers to me.

"Tonight's the night, yeah?" calls Serge over the music, his gold cross bouncing.

"Tonight's the night!" I shout back. Natasha smiles her sphinx-y quarter smile, which either means she's in or she's out. I've given up trying to read Natasha. She doesn't let anyone too close. Dance is what our friendship, if that's what you can call it, is built upon. In Marin, she'd pick me up from my Friday-night job at IHOP, and we'd speed into San Francisco to dance for two days straight at the gay clubs. On Mondays, we'd be back in the college jazz studio, having exchanged about twenty words the whole weekend.

Around midnight, Natasha retreats to her closet-size bedroom and comes back out wearing baggy black dance pants, a handkerchief wrapped around her thick black curls, black jazz dance shoes, and a black puffer—the same outfit I've changed into—and the three of us take the Q to the place Serge has been gushing about since the second he met us: Club Shelter. It's nothing special from the outside, a throbbing brick box surrounded by burned-out warehouses on Hubert Street in lower Manhattan. "You'll see," Serge says as we approach. Leading us to an unmarked entrance on the side of the building, he points out a muscular, dreadlocked guy in crisp jeans and a skintight T-shirt, unloading crates of records from a double-parked Toyota 4Runner.

"The Maestro!" Serge whisper-shouts in my ear.

I widen my eyes, pretending I get the reference, and follow Serge into the lofty space, where we each hand a petite woman with a shaved head and Hula-Hoop earrings our hard-earned fifteen dollars.

A foreign beat wraps around us as we make our way toward the crowd that rolls like the sea under blue and green lights. Natasha drifts away, and Serge beckons me to follow him deeper into the water, but I wave him off, leaning against a pillar, listening. A burst of heavy strings. A drum break. A gospel choir breaks into euphoric song. At the San Francisco clubs, it was all house and rap. This music is something else—hypnotic.

The people here—mostly young Black and Hispanic men—aren't just regular clubbers on a Saturday night, they're the best street dancers I've ever seen. And I work with some pretty great ones at EJM. I'm still a beginner at breakdancing, but I've been learning the basics, enough to know that what I'm watching takes breaking to a whole new level—make that a whole new dimension. Every dancer on the floor has a unique style, each infusing their moves with different degrees and combinations of jazz, ballet, modern, Latin, disco, you name it. Somehow, they all move together in a pattern, wordlessly communicating. Every time the beat drops, the house lights go black and all the dancers jump into the air at the same exact moment. Every time, I gasp with astonishment.

One guy, brown-skinned and lithe, stands out above all the rest. A street dancer with classical flair, he pirouettes faster than any ballerina I've ever seen. He feels me looking and smiles. I shock myself by smiling back, not looking away. The dancer weaves his way toward me, the crowd parting for him.

He reaches for my hand, which automatically floats up to meet his. With a featherlight gesture, he signals me closer.

"You know the Hustle?" His breath is warm and weedy in my ear.

Everyone in my family knows the Hustle. It's the Tylers' favorite dance besides the Lindy. "Sure," I say. A red strobe passes, hopefully camouflaging my blush.

The dancer's eyebrows arch. He probably thinks—given I'm a white girl, one of the few in the place—that I know the *Saturday Night Fever*, finger-pointing-at-the-sky version of the dance. I do know that version; we teach it to the kids at bar mitzvahs. But I also know the partner Hustle that my aunts and uncles did at family parties, closer to a tango, closer to sex.

"I'm Jesús," the dancer yells.

"Hi!" I wave like a cheerleader, all bubbly and uncool.

"What's your name?"

"Kimberly!"

Usually, I lie to the guys I meet at clubs, but no part of me feels the need to do that with this one. Still, I don't want to try to talk. I want to dive into this joy I've somehow found myself at the edge of, so I take the lead, pulling Jesús deeper into the sea. He laughs and follows me in. A new DJ is just taking over, to wild applause. Peering into the shadowy rafters, I see it's the guy from outside, the Maestro, bending over a turntable, dreadlocks swaying. Magnetic.

As the beat transitions from Afro to Latin, Jesús touches the small of my back, and we press together, breaking into a rhythmic two-step, our bodies effortlessly in sync. On a small stage to our left, dancers circle around an ecstatic woman, shaking cowbells to the beat. The woman bows out and a capoeira guy jumps into the ring, flipping backward on one hand. Next, a beautiful Japanese American woman jumps in, douses the floor with talcum powder, and launches into an acrobatic lofting routine that would put any Olympic gymnast to shame. Only, I don't sense an ounce of the brittle competitiveness that I felt between gymnasts at competitions. Just love and acceptance. Just one human being after another, leaping into the circle, showing off their best moves, then springing out, to applause and hugs. I wish they'd hug me, too. They're just a bunch of strangers, but I feel connected to each and every one of them.

I can't wait to write to Aunt Pat and describe this feeling. *Weightless* is the word I'll use.

Please do not take this safety away. Please let me stay here, forever.

As if he's heard my prayer, Jesús holds up a bright blue pill, pinching it delicately between his fingertips—a priest offering a tiny communion wafer.

I stick out my tongue.

7

THE ART OF
SELF-SABOTAGE

2001
Twenty-four years old

"Five, six, seven, eight!" Ms. Kelly smacks her wooden pointer in her open palm, keeping time as she stalks back and forth across the studio. We're doing rapid-fire *grand battements* at the barre, loosening our hips. Or the other girls are. I'm not really here.

It's 8:15 AM on a Monday. The last time I was inside my body was about six hours ago, at Club Shelter. Six hours ago, I was popping and locking and spinning on my back in a cloud of baby powder, circled by stunning, sweaty, shirtless men. Six hours ago, my heart was bursting with rainbow-colored love. I was one with everyone in that room, with the city, the dawn, the universe! I was the girl who got away. I was out of my head on ecstasy.

After that, as the sun rose over Brooklyn, I was floating up to my bathroom ceiling, watching Jesús have sex with me against the sink.

Now, there's a dry hole where that rainbow was. I'm dancing like a zombie with cement blocks for feet.

The Ailey School is one of the best dance schools in the world, and somehow they let me in. My looks don't draw attention to me here, like at Shelter, where they call me La Jirafa, "the Giraffe." In fact, my whiteness erases me at this famously diverse school. I like it that way. Why would I want to draw attention to the fact that even on my best days, I'm not as good as the others?

I look around at my perfectly-in-step classmates with their immaculate, glossy buns and pristine tights and unbelievable posture. Then there's me, in the studio mirror—bloodshot raccoon eyes, ashy skin, parched yellow hair. I turn away in disgust. *What's next, meth?*

"Kimberly!" snaps Ms. Kelly, jolting me back. "Your articulation is sloppy!"

My face burns with embarrassment, but the rest of my body lights up in a good way. My arm floats, my spine stretches, my muscles shift into alignment. I'm here for the humiliation. The general ballet ethos—that our bodies are hostile forces, enemies to be disciplined and starved and controlled—gels perfectly with how I like to treat myself. I've been punishing my body for its crimes since way before I knew what they were.

Bring it on, Ms. Kelly.

Right on cue, she appears at my side, pointing her stick at my chest. The outline of my nipple ring is showing through my black leotard. *"Take it out,"* she stage-whispers.

I nod, crisp as a soldier.

"And practice your *dégagés*," Ms. Kelly adds, continuing down the line.

Dégager is French for disengage, as in "I disengaged from my life a long time ago." In ballet, the *dégagé* leads to the kick of the *grand battement*. It's the moment when the working leg separates from the standing one and the floor. As with every-thing in ballet, it's more intricate than it looks. You can't do it on autopilot, but you can't overthink it, either.

I shift forward on my standing foot and my working foot rotates, brushing—toe, ball, heel—lightly from the floor. *Dégagé* to *grand battement* to fifth position to *dégagé* to *grand battement* to fifth position . . . I'm just starting to flow when the studio door opens and a skinny kid walks in. With a glance at Ms. Kelly, he sits at the piano in the corner. My heart sinks. We've gone without a pianist all semester, but it seems they've found one. As he begins to play, cold sweat prickles my neck.

Keep your shit together. You cannot have a flashback here.

Too late.

I'm not in the studio anymore. I'm in the basement, under the player piano, hunched against the redbrick wall. "Rag-time"—to cover my noises—vibrates in my spine. Sawdust itches my nose. I hear whistling, see his black leather work shoes pacing the length of the piano, taunting me. I push deeper into the corner, bury my face. Any second now he'll reach under and—

"*Pssst!*"

A girl with a high swirling bun motions for me to turn around. I'm back at the barre. We switched sides? My face is wet with tears, my breath ragged. I swipe at my cheeks and pivot the other way, dazed. Is he gone? I whip my gaze around the studio. No demons, just a blurry wash of pink and all-shades-of-brown arms sweeping into fifth position. That kid is still at the piano. The notes sound muffled and faraway, but the room is coming back into focus. Did I make a fool of myself? How long was I facing the wrong way? Did I cry out?

Ms. Kelly claps her hands three times. "Turns across the floor!"

I turn toward the door. I don't want to do *chaîné* turns out in the open, I want to slink out of here and never come back. Why push myself so hard when I'll never outrun him, never outsmart him?

Because we're Marines, goddammit! shouts Dad's voice in my head.

I get back in line, keep moving till the piano stops.

In the changing room, I lock myself in a bathroom stall and crouch into the little space by the toilet. Now that I've stopped dancing, my body doesn't know what else to do but shake and leak tears. I hug myself, trying to stop it—at least long enough to get out of the building without drawing more attention. I should be able to do that much. I'm a grown-up now, not that little girl in the basement.

Fuck that girl.

She knew things, she must have. When she was safe at home in Mom's arms, why didn't she tell? Everything could have been different.

...

At home, I shower and rub the steamy bathroom mirror with my towel. I can see my ribs, and my stomach is growling, which means it's okay to eat dinner tonight. I'll order Chinese from Kam Tak. But first, I have other business with this body. I've laid out my tools on the vanity: needle-nose pliers, cotton balls, hydrogen peroxide.

The piercing in my nipple is an open circle, clasped with a round bead. It's called a captive bead ring. I've heard women say their nipple piercings heighten their sensitivity in an erotic way. But mine just plain hurts. Most of the time, the ache is dull. When I have my period, it's sharp as a bite.

I did this to myself when I was eighteen, after the belly button ring and string of holes running up my earlobe. Now I'm going to undo it.

"Thank you, Ms. Kelly," I say to the mirror, wrenching the ring apart. The bead clinks into the sink, rolls down the drain. "And also, fuck you."

When Serge and Natasha get home, I'm hunched over the kitchen table, scraping out the insides out of my egg rolls and refilling the greasy shells with fried rice. I got two orders—six supersize rolls—a reward for being not only thin enough, not only hungry enough, but hurting enough.

Serge drops his dance bag and leans over my spread. "Girl, what are you doing?"

"Don't ask!" calls Natasha, disappearing into her room.

"They have less calories this way," I tell Serge matter-of-factly, though this is not exactly a fact, just another food rule I've made up because it works for me.

"*Okaaayyy*," he says, clicking a CD into the boom box.

A spot of red is seeping through my shirt. I hunch over more to hide it, reaching for the second clamshell of eggrolls. This will definitely push me over my daily calorie limit. I'll have to roll back the count in the bathroom later, which is depressing. I was doing so well. It's been six whole days since I purged. I call it bulimia now. It's not just about killing him anymore; it's also about killing fat.

Be kind to your body, says a gentle voice in my head. Aunt Pat. I picture her cross-legged, like the Buddha, which is how she looks now—rounded out by age and self-acceptance. *Your body is your temple*, she reminds me. *If you don't take care of it, you'll never be able to take care of anybody else.*

I push the container to the edge of the table. I can make a different choice. I did it once already today. I didn't run away after my flashback. I found my stronger place. What if I just kept doing that?

"Take those," I tell Serge. "I got them for you."

We both know Serge only eats the veggie chow fun from Kam Tak, but he whisks the rolls away without a word, confirming himself as an actual living saint.

8

CRASHING IN
SLO-MO

2002
Twenty-five years old

Kim,

Before you lie your most critical choices: to thrive or
merely exist; to live or die; to feel or freeze; to fight
or flee.

Do not avoid your suffering. Feel it and let it go!
Stay interested in everything that comes next—it
is the true path to healing. Although it is painful
to relive traumatic events, it is the antidote to a life
unlived, devoid of passion.

Bring breath to the pain. Snuggle next to it, as a
love. Look closely into the eyes of it. Be with it, for
what it is.

I love you with popping eyeballs,

Aunt Pat

Aunt Pat, my pen pal, my savior. Ever since my memories began to surface, I've been writing her long letters—asking questions about her father, detailing my memories, letting them out, trying to let them go. She always answers, encouraging me to push on, but rarely does she talk about herself. It was only recently that Aunt Pat confirmed it to me: she, too, was a victim.

The year was 1952, and Aunt Pat was nine when she told Grandma Gen what her father had been doing to her late at night in her bed. He denied it, of course. "I was just pulling up the covers," he lied. Grandma Gen believed him, she claims. Either way, he stopped visiting Aunt Pat's bedroom after she told on him. It was like it never happened.

Only it did. And it kept on happening, to others in our extended family. How many others? With so much secrecy in the Tyler clan, we'll never know. The stories I *have* heard are incredibly painful—and not mine to tell. Most of his victims are unhappy that I'm open about my own past. But keeping quiet was never an option. Mom and Aunt Pat have always understood this. As private as they are, they've learned the hard way: silence and repression don't work.

"If I'd never told Grandma Gen," Aunt Pat once said to Mom, "he would've kept coming to my room, and the rest of you might have been spared."

"Don't you dare put that on yourself," Mom told her.

But Aunt Pat can't help it. She's our vessel, our pain carrier, and we are a heavy burden.

Dear Aunt Pat,

I did yoga, like you suggested! It was Bikram style—hot. I got a spot in the corner where I felt protected. The class was ninety minutes long and consisted of twenty-six postures that you repeated two times each. There were breathing exercises where you clasped a hand to your throat, inhaled, put your head back, and released everything in a whoosh. I felt so out of my body, I thought I might have a panic attack. It was amazing, though.

I remember you once told me the throat chakra represents the ability to speak and communicate clearly, and the throat is where childhood abuse survivors hold a lot of their pain. The truths we couldn't speak as children get stuck there. I feel mine coming unstuck.

Love,

Kimberly

I try to sound optimistic in my letters. I keep it to myself that as much as I want to thrive, I don't believe I deserve to—and I still can't picture myself living past thirty. Not that I'm suicidal, I'm just too busy surviving.

Some things I don't share with Aunt Pat because, even at the selfish age of twenty-five, I understand that she can carry

only so much. Also, I can't stand the idea that she might secretly think less of me. She doesn't have to know I've spent
the last few years sleeping around a fair amount, once waking
up naked beside a total stranger. She doesn't have to know
about the drugs or the crack house–style New Jersey hotels
Jesús used to take me to after Club Shelter. And she doesn't
have to know that I ran out and got an AIDS test the other
morning (negative!) after waking up in a cold panic that I
could have it—and kill my new boyfriend. Or vice versa.

My new boyfriend is the Maestro, whose actual name is
Timmy. He's good for me, in more ways than not. He's thirty-
eight, a real grown-up, with a real purpose for getting up in
the morning—by far the most successful person I've ever been
with. By day, he's the vice president of A&R at Dreamworks
Records. By night, he's a composer, musician, and DJ. Now
that Club Shelter is my real home, I understand why everyone
there idolizes him. Timmy's spiritually tinged house music
gives us something sacred, a sense of belonging. Still, no one,
not even me, knows him. Timmy likes it that way, so I don't
mind that he asks me to keep our relationship a secret. It's a
fair trade-off for the things he gives me: stability, guidance, a
sense of possibility.

I love my friends at Shelter, but they're struggling, too.
Everyone at Shelter can dance. Like me, everyone *says* they
want to be a famous dancer. But then we're too hungover
from doing ecstasy or acid or the combo, candy flippin', to
make auditions the next day. The fact that I'm with someone
like Timmy makes me want to do better, and I'm starting to.
On Sunday nights, at least, I stick to dancing on Rip Fuel, a

caffeine and ephedrine pill. Monday mornings, I show up to Ailey with clean tights, clean hair, and my head on mostly straight.

Timmy doesn't have *all* the power in our relationship. Right from the start, when he sent his assistant down to the dance floor to get my number and I sent the guy back empty-handed, I've held my own. That's why I'm not like the others, why I have my own drawer in his dresser, my toothbrush in his medicine cabinet: I made the Maestro come to me.

On our first date, he took me to the kind of dark and twinkly restaurant I never thought I'd see from the inside. "You should come over," he said, shattering the top of our crème brûlée with a tap of his spoon. "We'll play some records."

Cut to Timmy's prewar apartment in Gramercy Park. Me, acting unimpressed with his marble countertops and hardwood floors and real furniture that he definitely didn't assemble with an Allen key. The place was sparkling clean, with no decorations on the walls except for a dozen or so gold records from artists produced by Timmy: Boyz II Men, New Edition, Patti LaBelle, Johnny Gill, Erik B. & Rakim. . . . I wandered into a room filled only with crates of albums, turntables, recording equipment, and a single leather armchair.

"Go ahead, put something on," Timmy said, handing me a glass of water that I wished was a real drink. I picked a still-in-the-wrapper single with a black cross on the cover. It was so good I played it over and over, dancing around the music room while Timmy watched from the armchair with an unreadable smile.

"Don't you love it?" I yelled, twirling.

Timmy shrugged. "Not really."

"Are you kidding me? It's amazing! You *need* to play this at the club. Promise me you'll play it Saturday night. Promise!"

"I don't make promises," said Timmy.

But he did play the record that Saturday at Shelter, and people loved it, just like I said they would. They loved it so much he played it twice in a row—something Timmy only does rarely, when a track takes the crowd to next-level states of euphoria. Having the Maestro play a song that *I* discovered not once, but twice, was an honor, an anointment. I had Timmy's respect after that.

Sex is always easy for me in the beginning of a relationship. As long as I'm in control, and there's no love involved, I'm in my comfort zone. And there's no real danger of Timmy loving me. The Maestro can have any woman he wants, so I say nothing when he does. Who am I to want more? Likewise, I've learned it's better not to talk to Timmy about my memories, or to see him at all if I'm in a dark place after a flashback. Timmy supports me, he encourages me, he even paid for me to go to the dentist and get my cracked tooth fixed—but he doesn't want to hear about my past.

"My childhood wasn't a picnic, either," Timmy will say. "But that's behind me now. I prefer to live in the present."

He makes it sound like a choice, but for me it isn't. My past is always waiting to pounce and take me down. A passerby wearing Old Spice, a pretty map in a gift shop, sawdust on a bar floor, cocktail stirrers, clocks ticking, the chill of wet hair on my back . . . . That's only a partial list of my triggers, the seemingly harmless things I must avoid to survive daily life.

What's even worse is that sometimes—I don't know why, but especially when things are going well for me—I seek my triggers out.

...

My heart beats faster with every mile that closes between my little red Honda and JFK Airport, where I'm headed to pick up Timmy. He's been in Japan for two weeks to DJ, and I've missed him. I can't wait to jump into his strong arms, wrap my legs around his waist, and kiss him right out in the open. He'll allow it, because airports are full of strangers. Timmy loves traveling. He says one day he'll take me to Japan with him, and we'll eat sushi even better than they have at Nobu, his favorite restaurant. I find that impossible to believe, but then I'd never even tasted sushi before I met Timmy, so who knows what I don't know?

Fumbling in my purse on the seat next to me, I pull out a beat-up cassette tape that I only listen to when Timmy's not around to make fun of me: the Indigo Girls' *Rites of Passage*. I click it into the player and crank the volume till the speakers pop and crackle.

"How long till my soul gets it right?" I'm shouting with the music at the top of my lungs, so carried away by the song that I don't realize what I'm doing till I've already done it: I've just taken the Rockville Centre exit off the LIE. A minute ago, I was flying away from my pain, now I'm detouring, intentionally, toward it. How fucked up is that? But here I am, speeding past the Rockville Links Club and turning onto Earle Avenue, with its stone-cold mini mansions, protected behind walls of evergreens and boxwood hedges.

Just a quick drive-by, I tell myself.

Across from the house, I pull over, eject the Indigo Girls, and glower. Grandma Gen followed her daughters to Marin years ago, but I slouch low in my seat, half expecting her to burst out the front door. The place has had a makeover, but even with cheerful daffodils in the window boxes, it looks like its old lying self to me. It looks like her.

Today is the last day of March. Easter Sunday, in fact. We always came on Easter—Collette and me in our pink suits and white hats, heads hanging as we followed Mom's high heels up the redbrick walk. I step on the gas.

Not that I ever doubted the curse of Earle Avenue, but five minutes later, waiting to turn left at the Seaman Avenue light, I get to see it in action. A gray Lexus is speeding straight for the intersection, the red light, me. I lock eyes with the terrified teenage boy behind the wheel as he crashes into my driver's-side door. Metal crunches into my hip; glass rains everywhere.

My eyelids scrape open and closed, open and closed. I drift in and out. Through my broken window, I glimpse the boy running, stumbling, toward me. "Are you alright? Oh my God, oh my God, are you okay?" he shouts. I turn my head away. An ambulance wails quietly, then louder. Men in yellow suits and red hats appear, pulling the kid away, yelling at me to stay calm, something about the jaws of life. One of them aims a metal pincher at my door. "Don't try to move!" he commands.

But I'm already wrenching my left leg free of the crunched-in metal around it. "It's okay, I got it," I burble, pulling myself across the passenger seat to unlock the door. *Good*, I think, just before passing out in the man's arms. *Someone's going to fix me now.*

In the ambulance, I wake to a blurry-faced EMT dabbing my face with a cold cloth. My contact lenses have crumpled into hard pebbles, shoved deep into my eye sockets. I ask for a mirror, please, to take them out.

"I don't think you want a mirror right now," says the EMT. "If you can just hold on a little longer—"

"*Give me one!*" I snarl, surprising us both. Reluctantly, the EMT hands me a plastic mirror. Oh. My left eyelid appears to have met a meat grinder. I turn from side to side, smiling at myself. There's so much blood. Blood in my lashes; blood oozing from my nose, into my mouth. The sight is oddly comforting. I scrape out my crumpled lenses and hand the mirror back.

"Thank you so much," I say, remembering my manners.

At the hospital, a nurse wants to know who she should call for me. I ask her to call Timmy to tell him I won't be picking him up at the airport; and my dad, to come for me. Dad only lives a few miles from the hospital they brought me to, so he's the obvious choice, but part of me wonders if he'll show up. He doesn't approve of my lifestyle, my friends, my refusal to get a normal job and live a normal life.

But of course Dad comes. There's been a car accident, after all. A bona fide emergency.

He brings his new wife, Betsy, who I barely know. Through

my painkiller fog, I hear them discussing my X-rays with the doctor.

"Talk about Easter miracles," says the doctor, repeating the line he gave me a few minutes ago. "No broken bones, though she may have sustained some nerve damage to her legs. We're waiting on our plastic surgeon to stitch up the cuts on her face. The real blessing is she didn't lose that eye."

"Tell him to be careful with her face," I hear Betsy say. "She's a model."

I like her for that, but it's not true. I was looking into modeling, but it hasn't happened yet. I don't even have an agent. I can almost hear Dad thinking, *She's no model; she's a bar mitzvah dancer.*

I don't mind. Eight hours and dozens of stitches later, as Dad carries me from his truck into the house he shares with Betsy, I melt into his strong arms. He's taking care of me, the way I always wanted.

9

PORTRAITS OF DENIAL

2002

Twenty-five years old

Mom called me every day after the accident, checking on my progress and distracting me with funny stories about her new day-care business while I white-knuckled it through physical therapy "exercises"—invisible-to-the-eye leg lifts and hip stretches. One day, when I answered, crying in frustration, she said, "That's it, I'm flying you here. There's no better place to heal than Marin." Which might be true.

It's easier to move as slowly as I do in a place where time itself seems slowed down, where no one's in a rush and people don't bump you on the sidewalks because there hardly *are* sidewalks, just winding roads and quiet park trails. It's peaceful, being wrapped in nature. But even more therapeutic is Mom's concern. She's never been this worried about me, not even the time when I got run over by a limo at high school prom and broke my leg all kinds of ways. I've finally done it: found a way to show her. Never have I felt so seen.

Aunt Pat has been healing me with her magic hands. She's now a certified massage therapist, lucky for me. Thanks to our daily bodywork sessions, I'm starting to walk better, though with a pretty dramatic limp. The doctors in New York said I might not dance again, but they're wrong. They also said I might only walk from my bed to the bathroom and back for several months. But this morning, I hiked a slow mile through the redwoods with Aunt Pat.

Now I'm lying under a white sheet on a massage table in her bodywork studio—a sunny converted woodshed behind her home. Aunt Pat still lives in the hills of Marin, but in a smaller, humbler house than the one she shared with Aunt Shawn. I cried when they broke up a few years ago. Still, I'm glad Aunt Pat moved. I can't separate my memories of their old house in Lagunitas from Aunt Kristy's engagement party, when I was eight.

"You've got goose bumps!" says Aunt Pat, releasing her hands from my thigh. She pulls down the sheet to cover me. "Let me get a blanket."

"No, Aunt Pat, I'm fine," I say, focusing on the warm slant of sunlight across my bare throat and shoulders. "Please, keep going. It's helping."

"Okay. Just breathe," Aunt Pat says softly. Her hands move to my face, tenderly pressing the ropy ridges over my left eye. "I know it hurts, but if we don't break up this tissue, you'll have some pretty big keloid scars."

Aunt Pat has explained to me that traumatic memories live not only in our brains but in our skin, muscles, cells, and even our hormones. The work we're doing, she says, can help my body let go of emotional knots as well as physical ones. As her hands move from my face to my aching left arm, I imagine the knots unraveling inside me, poisonous vapor rising from my skin. Tears roll down my cheekbones and pool inside my ears.

When we're through, Aunt Pat kneels on a maroon cushion before her little altar in the corner of the room and lights a bundle of sage with a match. I don't mind the earthy, sweaty smell because it's always reminded me of her. Aunt Pat says sage clears out bad energy and brings in the good. She places the smoking twigs in a little dish on the altar, and I kneel beside her, touching each of her sacred items, like I used to when I was little. There's the same roly-poly stone Buddha that I remember, but the offerings at his feet have changed.

Not long after her father died, Aunt Pat went to a spiritual retreat and didn't speak for a whole week and shaved off all of her hair, which had grown long. After that, Grandma Gen's rosary beads and the Catholic prayer for healing were removed from the altar—replaced with a brass bowl that moans when you circle it with a wooden mallet, an assortment of dried ferns and flowers from her hikes, a silky cream scarf that Aunt Pat calls a "kata," and a laminated card listing the Five Precepts of Buddhism:

I accept the precept of no killing.
I accept the precept of no stealing.

I accept the precept of no sexual abuse.

I accept the precept of no dishonesty.

I accept the precept of no alcohol and drugs.

Aunt Pat says the Precepts are comparable to the Ten Commandments of Christianity, except they're written in many different ways, and you don't go to hell for not following them. They seem like common sense to me, even the one about alcohol and drugs, which have lost their appeal since the accident. And while I wonder why anyone would need to be reminded not to commit sexual abuse, I guess it's good that the Buddhists spell it out in plain language. If the Catholics did, too, I wonder, would it have stopped him?

It's time to head back to Mom's. I refasten my necklace, an amethyst ice drop hanging from a crown on a fine gold chain. Aunt Pat gave it to me a long time ago, before I had my memories. Amethyst was extremely protective and soothing, she explained, knowing as always just what I needed. Now, she presses a tiny, handmade paper box into my hands. "Keep this with you," she says. "When you're sad, take one out—then go find that thing!"

I open the box to find a dozen or so little slips of paper, each with a single word written in Aunt Pat's hand: *cinema, food, fun, friends, allies.* . . .

The box is light as a bird's egg. I tuck it carefully into my puffer coat pocket. "Thank you. I'll always keep it."

"Good!" Aunt Pat's forehead furrows as she helps me down the sloping driveway to my car.

"What's wrong, Aunt Pat?"

"Nothing is wrong," she says, in her even, careful way. "Everything is just as it should be. I was only thinking . . . How would you feel about paying a visit to Grandma Gen—you, your mom, and me?"

My neck cinches up. It was loose as honey a second ago. I haven't talked to Grandma Gen since I moved back to New York after college. She sends me cards on my birthday, always with scripture printed in gold foil, prayers for my happiness, and a check for two hundred dollars. Every year, I glance at her generic note, pocket the cursed check, rip the card in half.

"Why?" I ask Aunt Pat.

"I think she's ready to hear you and your mom—about Grandpapa."

"Really?" I ask.

There's a part of me, fragile as Aunt Pat's origami box, that wonders if Grandma Gen doesn't truly understand what he did. This small part of me thinks that if she did, surely she'd take us more seriously, stop making excuses for him, choose *us*. It's the same, stubborn little part that whispers, *This will be the year she apologizes*, as I open her birthday card every year.

"Do you think it'll be different this time?" I ask Aunt Pat.

"I can't promise that," she says. "But your grandma's trying."

Trying is new. Trying is a start.

. . .

I can't stand being late, even when I dread where I'm going. Being late makes me feel out of control, which makes me feel unsafe. I arrive at Grandma Gen's condo fifteen minutes early, feeling unsafe anyway.

She opens the door with that big bubbly smile and all the layers of makeup and jewelry. Registering my face, she winces. "Oh, you look a sight!" A tiny, spotted gremlin pogoes at her high heels, yapping.

I jut out my chin, smirking a tiny bit. I wore no cover-up today, made no attempt to mask the tie-dye of bruises around my eyes, the hot pink scars on my forehead. If nothing else comes of our meeting, at least I got to gross her out.

Grandma Gen pats her teased silver hair. "I was just making lemonade!" *Don't you always.* She bends to pick up the gremlin, who stops barking long enough to lick her on the mouth. "Good girl, Lovey!" Grandma Gen coos. Lovey is what she used to call *him.*

I follow Grandma Gen inside, trying not to look at the anniversary portrait in the hall, my horrible childhood distilled in a tacky, gilded frame. I prepared for this moment. I was going to walk right by, not even glance at it. But I can't help myself. I lean in to study the girl in the frame—her lacy white dress, her red satin sash, her frozen grimace as she pees, invisibly for the moment, on her favorite aunt's lap.

Who is she? Is she me? Could we be the same person?

No. She's just a ghost, like him.

In the kitchen, Grandma Gen fusses around, stirring sugar into her silver wedding pitcher, washing her lemon press, disinfecting her granite countertops. Anything to keep her back turned to me. It's fine. I don't want to look at her face, either. On a brighter note, Grandma Gen has shrunk. All Tyler women are on the tall side, but I now stand a head above the one who used to tower over me in her grand entryway, looking for imperfections. I never had any visible ones, thanks to Mom's dedication to appearances. Never a hair out of place, never a spot to be found on my sparkling white tights. Until we left, that is.

"Here you go, dear!" Grandma Gen says. As she hands me my lemonade, one of her gold chains swings loose from her blouse, the pendant clinking against the crystal tumbler. His wedding ring, around her neck.

This is trying? What'll she bust out next? The I LOVE MY HUSBAND mug? Why am I even here? Why do I care what she has to say anymore? Aunt Pat thinks we'll speak our truths and be okay. But the truth is this: *we*, our family, will never be okay. Not unless each of us finds our own way to walk through our pain and come out on the other side, whole. The odds of that are not looking good.

"Kath says you're trying to model," says Grandma Gen. "Good for you!"

I sip my lemonade (bitter, of course) and weigh my next words. I could tell her that modeling was never a serious option, though she isn't the first person in our family to have latched on to the idea. I could put her on the spot: *Why is it that you value illusions over truth?* But instead, I say, "I'm looking for a better job. To pay for therapy."

Grandma Gen narrows her purple eyelids, and for one surreal second, I think she's going to address the therapy situation.

Soon after Mom had her first memories and read *The*

Courage to Heal, she gathered up her strength and asked her mother to pay for counseling. After much back and forth, it was agreed that the cost would be deducted from the balance of a loan Mom's parents had given her and Dad to buy our house. That's how Mom paid for my short-lived therapy in high school, too. But by the time I was in college and ready to try talking to someone again, the loan was repaid in full, the recovery fund dissolved. "I've done enough," Grandma Gen told Mom, who'd seen that coming for miles.

It was one thing for Grandma Gen to passively make reparations, quite another for her to actively do so. Writing Mom a check every month would be a regular reminder of what she'd devoted her life to forgetting.

"Hopefully that scar heals up," says Grandma Gen, circling back to the superficial, "if you want to take the modeling seriously."

I make a face to her back. "Hopefully," I say.

When the doorbell rings, she nearly trips over Lovey, racing to answer it.

In Grandma Gen's overstuffed living room, Mom takes a purple velvet armchair; Aunt Pat, who likes staying close to the earth, kneels beside her; and Grandma Gen and I perch at opposite ends of her rose-patterned sofa. Given how my one-on-one time with Grandma Gen went, I no longer hold much hope that she'll listen openheartedly to what we have to say, or confess why she let him get away with it, let alone say the two simple words we—especially Mom—need to hear.

As always, Aunt Pat starts the conversation. "Mom, Kim has some things she wants to talk to you about, if you will listen."

"Well, I'm here aren't I?" says Grandma Gen, with a hard little laugh at the end.

Why waste time? I dive right in. "Grandma, I don't know if you understand the severity of what he did to me."

She stares at me, her face an unreadable mask. I want to rip it off and see if there's blood and bone and tissue under there, or just a bunch of circuits. I want to shock her, shake her. "He made me do horrible things with him, Grandma Gen. Over and over. Every week."

Silence from Grandma Gen.

"It started when I was a baby, two or three, I think." I jab my thumb into the sorest spot on my bad hip to stay present. "Does that surprise you?"

She doesn't answer. She doesn't move, or blink. I might as well be talking to the wax Queen Elizabeth on her throne at Madame Tussauds. Mom, on the other hand, is sliding lower and lower into her chair, gripping a throw pillow like a shield to her heart. Aunt Pat puts a hand on Mom's thigh, nodding that I should continue.

"Do you remember when you found me soaking wet on the stairs, in the middle of the night? He made me shower with him." My voice sharpens with every word. Good. I hope I cut her.

"He loved special occasions, when I was in a dress," I go on. *Make her bleed.* "Did you know he raped me on my first communion, Grandma Gen?"

———

He'd just given me the boom box with the silver bow. I left
it on the grass, playing "We Are the World," to run to the
bathroom, upstairs. When I came out, tiptoeing toward my
bedroom to change into my favorite blue skirt (it was now
too short, but the wrap belt still protected me), he appeared
from the shadows, blocking my path. "What are you running
from?" he asked, and I heard a voice inside, loud and clear:
From you.

It happened in front of my dolls; I was still wearing my
communion dress and my new gold cross necklace with a diamond at the center, a gift from Mom and Dad. He said, "I'm
doing this to you because you're the prettiest one," and a new
kind of pain ripped me open. I rose up and watched myself on
my bed, screaming into his hand.

In Grandma Gen's living room, Mom sobs into her throw
pillow, but her mother is frozen behind her mask. All I care
about is smashing it. I have to try, at least. "Did you know he
gave me herpes, Grandma Gen? I was eight! He said, 'I'm
giving this to you,' like it was a present." This, too, I have
unfortunately remembered.

My grandmother scoffs, throwing up her hands. "Well, *I*
don't have herpes."

I stand up too fast, toppling against the sofa arm. Righting
myself, I face her. "Are you saying I'm lying?"

Grandma Gen won't look at me. She stiffens straighter,

tilts her head, and says, dryly, "I've never called you a liar, have I? I've always believed you."

"Don't you think that's a little strange?" I snap. I'm pacing now, each step a burst of clarifying pain. "If someone were to tell me my dad did what he did, I'd say they had to be lying!" Lovey rushes to my heels, yapping.

Ever the mediator, Aunt Pat cuts in. "Kath?" she says, gently pulling the pillow from Mom's wet face. "Is there anything you'd like to say?"

Mom just buckles, falls to the floor, releasing an eerie, primal wail—her trapped spirit, finally breaking free? I watch in shock as she crawls to Grandma Gen's feet, looking up at her mother with such naked, unbearable need that I start to turn away, but catch myself. I won't do what they did. *I see you in there, Mom. I see you like you could never see me.*

It's dawning on me: Mom was a little girl, once, just as I was. A little girl who was let down by her mother. Only, she had it worse, so much worse. *Her* mother knew. Grandma Gen protected him, knowingly. Kept Mom and Aunt Pat hostage to him. How did Mom survive that? How has she not buckled sooner? And how can I help her, now that she has? I want to throw my arms around her. But some part of me understands that, in spite of all appearances, she wouldn't want me to. This moment is between her and Grandma Gen.

"What do you want from me?" says Grandma Gen.

"All I ever wanted," rasps Mom, still on her hands and knees, "was an apology."

"Kath, I have apologized."

"No." Mom shakes her head. "No you never have."

"Okay, then." Grandma Gen actually shrugs. "I'm sorry."

The room falls silent.

"Kath, Mom," says Aunt Pat. "Should we take a breath, revisit this another time?"

Lifting her head from the floor, Mom musters a nod.

Grandma Gen has clearly given us all she can: she has allowed us to say these horrible things about her beloved Edward Royall. She hasn't called us liars. Hasn't kicked us out. It may be the closest to human I've ever seen her get. But it's not close enough. She rushes out to walk Lovey, followed by Aunt Pat, whose forgiveness knows no bounds.

"Mom?" I call up the stairs. "Let's go—before she gets back!"

There's no answer.

The last place on earth I want to go is upstairs, near Grandma Gen's bedroom, but Mom's been in the bathroom for fifteen minutes. I'm getting a panicky feeling, like I've turned my back in a store and lost a child. What if she needs my help?

Warily, I hobble up to the second floor.

"Mom?"

"In here."

I find her in a small cluttered room, a silver picture frame shaking in her hands. She is all I register, at first. "I was just looking at this," she says, holding out the frame. Inside is a faded snapshot of Mom as a little girl, smiling with her father under a grand old maple tree.

"Okay," I say. "We need to go now."

This is when I notice we're standing in a shrine. Other than a dozen or so QVC dress bags laid out on a purple day-bed, the room is devoted to him. Grandma Gen hasn't just held on to the anniversary portrait and his wedding ring. She's kept it all. His architecture awards on their little brass plaques. His flags and war medals. The I GOT YOU, BABE sash from his coffin. His image plasters the walls and clutters the bookshelves. There he is, twirling Grandma Gen on a dance floor. There he is—poster-size!—grinning from the cockpit of a fighter plane in the war. There he is, father of the century, tying Aunt Pat's shoelace just before she ran a marathon.

I back against the doorframe. "What is this? Did you know about this?"

"Oh, yes," she says. "It's always been here."

Grandma Gen moved here more than a decade ago, just after Mom and I had our memories and everything came out. There was no denying who he was when she created this . . . monument.

"Please, Mom. We really need to—"

Mom nods, carefully returning the picture to a shelf. But she doesn't budge. Of all the lies surrounding us, she can't seem to turn away from this particular one.

Abruptly, she reaches out and knocks the frame on its face.

I'm proud of her, for the few seconds before she stands the girl and her father back up.

"*Take us home!*" I want to scream. But something tells me to keep my mouth shut. I can be patient, like Aunt Pat. I'm not the child here. And Kathy Murphy is definitely not the mother. But she's not that girl under the maple tree, either.

She's stronger than them both. I know this when, finally, she tips the frame for good.

...

Later, I'll hear the story: Before Earle Avenue, Mom's family lived in a smaller house, with the maple tree in front. Mom loved that tree. She would climb it every day after school, where the effort of trying to be perfectly invisible exhausted her. The higher she climbed, moving effortlessly from branch to branch, the more grounded she felt. Her body knew how to get to the top. She would sit there for hours, wrapped in the tree's strength, safe from fears that she couldn't understand. One spring day when she was twelve, the town came to chop down the tree in an effort to widen the street. Grandma Gen allowed Mom to climb it one last time before the chain saws arrived. For nearly an hour, as she crouched in the branches, trucks idled below. Then, a miracle: they left. Her father had promised to help the town redesign the street to save her tree.

After her memories, Mom would marvel at the absurdity of it: her father could fix anything, except himself.

10

STRIPPED

The Ailey School won't wait for me to heal. By the time I get back from California, my spot has been filled. The other toe shoe has dropped, as I always knew it would.

To cheer me up, Timmy takes me to Nobu. I usually love coming here. Raw fish is still a bit exotic for my taste, but I love the cold, dry sake and cucumber rolls and the birch tree sculptures that stretch up to the ceiling. It's nothing like the stuffy white-tablecloth and silver-gravy-boat restaurants I went to growing up, when *they* took us.

But tonight, I can't appreciate that; I'm not rising to the occasion. My hip is killing me; my bruises itch; I'm so broke that Timmy's been paying my rent; and, worst of all, today I got a letter from Aunt Pat, apologizing for Grandma Gen, as if it's *Aunt Pat* who should be sorry. I can't stop thinking,

What was that all for? Will we ever change? I put down my chopsticks and start to cry.

"White people are staring," Timmy quietly informs me. "They think you're crying because I hit you."

I roll my eyes, blotting them with my napkin. "That's ridiculous."

Then I look around. He's right. The woman at the next table raises her eyebrows at me in the universal girl signal for *Need backup?* I glare back at her.

Timmy laughs. "Welcome to my life, Twiggy. I told you—I deal with this every single day."

Twiggy is another name they call me at Shelter, after the model from the 1960s. We don't look that much alike, but she was blond and blue-eyed, and I'm the only blond, blue-eyed girl at the club. Which I'm beginning to realize is a lot more fun than being the only Black man in a Tribeca sushi restaurant. So *this* is what Timmy means when he says racism is everywhere, I just don't see it because I don't have to. I can't believe I made light of it when he told me he owns a car because a Black man can't get a cab in New York. "So how do you justify owning *three* cars?" I joked.

But I'm dead serious now. "Ignore them!" I say, straightening in my chair. "Idiots."

Timmy folds his napkin into a perfect triangle, places it next to his plate, and signals for the check, which appears instantly—the way everything Timmy asks for does. And not just because he's rich and sometimes famous. Timmy's cool, unimpressed gaze makes people—nonracist people, at least—want to impress him.

Now he's standing, pushing in his chair, leaving seventy-five dollars' worth of sashimi untouched on his plate, because these shitty strangers are silently blaming him for *my* bruises and *my* tears. Which won't seem to stop.

"Timmy, please?" I plead, sniffling. "Please sit down?"

Timmy shakes his head. "No drama, Twiggy. You know how I feel about drama."

I follow him outside, but he'll barely look at me. "I think you need to go home," he says, getting into his Jaguar. "Seems like you're pretty upset."

All night, tossing and thrashing on my futon, Timmy's voice replays in my head. *No drama, Twiggy. . . . Seems like you're pretty upset.* He sounded so tired—tired of me. He's pulling away. I'm too much, just like Dad always said.

I'd better figure out how to pay my own rent next month.

There's a girl I know at Shelter who strips at a new "gentlemen's club" in Midtown called Prestige. Sometimes she makes four hundred dollars a night in tips. Natasha and I used to talk—in a joking, desperate way—about auditioning. One time, for research, I went to a strip place here in Brooklyn. I sneaked backstage, where one of the "girls," who was probably in her late thirties, had pictures of her five-year-old daughter in a pink tutu taped to her dressing room mirror. The woman had Grandma Gen shades of purple eyeshadow right up to her eyebrows. She had red dots on her arms and legs that she dabbed with concealer. She said they were flea bites. She said this was one of her three jobs to make ends meet. She said she'd been stripping since her daughter was two, and there'd only been "trouble" with a couple of customers. That had been enough for me. I walked home in the middle of the dark, empty street with my keys in a knife grip, holding my breath.

But that was the old me, the "drama queen." I'm done with her endless emotions, her pointless hang-ups. *Your body's never been yours anyway. Why care who sees it?*

In the morning, I walk to Flatbush Avenue and spend the last fifty dollars on my credit card on some necessities: clear stiletto platform heels and a neon-pink thong and bra from the sticky-carpeted Rainbow Shop; and three mini bottles of tequila from the bodega, where G-Money, the drug dealer, is hanging by the door with the usual cast of weathered-looking guys in fake bling.

"Got one for me, Snowflake?" says one of them, pointing to my clear plastic bag.

"Sorry." I step around him. "I need them all."

He gets in my face, about to needle me, but G-Money shuts him down. "Leave her alone. That's the ballerina you're talking to." As I turn the corner, he calls after me, "You're gonna be a star—right, ballerina?"

I turn and give him a small smile. "Not quite."

...

All of us girls auditioning to be professional objects are funneled down a narrow flight of stairs, into a small basement room, like cattle down a chute and into a pen. The guy in charge of us looks the part, at least in my memory: goatee, beer belly, polyester shirt unbuttoned over a tank top, gold chains—the whole look. He tells us we'll each get two minutes on the "podium," the little round stage with the pole upstairs, where all the watery-eyed men are sitting with their watered-down drinks. After everyone is done, the boss explains, he'll come back to the cattle pen and tell us who made the cut. I look around at the other girls, a younger, healthier-looking bunch than at the Brooklyn club I scouted. How could any of us not make this cut? How hard can it be?

In a bathroom stall, I peel off my dance pants, step into the wobbly plastic stilettos, down my three tequilas, wincing, and try not to worry about what Aunt Pat would think. Outside in the pen, the other girls primp in near silence.

"Let's go!" calls the boss. We line up on the stairs in our mesh-and-lace getups, stony-faced as pallbearers, waiting for our turn. Looking around at the others, it hits me: all these girls have *boobs*. Boobs are everywhere. I look down at mine, in their tiny A-cups. Shit. I give them a push, but there's no getting them to look like the other girls'—no fresh-risen loaves in my bra.

It's okay, I tell myself. *They have boobs, but I have moves.* I doubt any of these women have trained at the Ailey School. If they had, why would they be doing this? *Good question, Kimberly.*

When I reach the front of the line and see the stage, my stomach drops through the grimy floor. The girl on the podium isn't just gyrating robotically around the pole. She's performing a tightly choreographed, *Flashdance*-style routine, tumbling

and leaping with impressive athleticism. Did I mention she's
topless?

What am I going to do out there? It won't be enough to
freestyle it like I do at Shelter, and clearly, the *tendus* and
chaîné turns I perfected at Ailey will not be coming in handy
today. As the girl onstage finishes her routine, reaching under her crotch-length skirt and shimmying out of her panties
with a wink, a hand on my back shoves me onto the stage.

Wobbling into the spotlight, I look at the floor and con-
centrate on the underwater bass notes of "Closer" by Nine
Inch Nails. "I wanna fuck you like an animal," sneers Trent
Reznor, as my body sways and launches itself into a hybrid of
modern, ballet, hip-hop, and Riverdance. I curl into a ball,
fling my arms wide, kick my leg so high I almost knock myself out. I haven't attempted the splits since my accident, but
what the hell, I grip the pole and drop. Both my ankles twist
as I land, but I hardly feel any pain. *Thanks, tequila!* Clamoring
to my feet, I remember: strippers have to take off their clothes.
Frowning, I reach back, unhook my bra, chuck it onto the
stage. A whistle from the faceless audience. "Lose the panties!"

It's not your body anyway, remember? I hook my thumbs over
the flimsy lace hips of my thong but can't bring myself to
tug downward. "Smile, baby!" taunts another voice. I can do
that. I learned from the best how to smile through anything.
Arranging my face into that familiar, tight shape, I force my
chin up and look out at the dim smoky room for the first time.
That's when I see him, the ghost of Christmases past, sitting
three feet away from the podium, leering up at me. And there
he is again, smoking at the bar. And over there, slowly stirring

his drink. I glance from table to table to table—seeing only
him, him, him.

Acid creeps up my throat and I swallow it, eyes tearing.

"I said, time's up!" yells the boss from somewhere behind me.

Did he? When did the song end? There's a long, mean silence as I snatch up my bra and sprint off the stage, heels
echoing after me.

You seriously failed at that? I think, trudging toward the subway.

I was somehow surprised, and kind of indignant, when I
wasn't chosen. I'd been unprepared, definitely. It didn't help
that my mind filled the place with *him*. But come on: *What
kind of dancer can't even make it as a stripper?*

On the Q train platform, I shove the slutty shoes into
an overstuffed garbage can and squeeze into a packed car.
Crushed against the doors, I put on my headphones and sum-
mon the Indigo Girls. "Fasten up your earthly burdens," they
sing, more heavenly than any church choir. "You have just
begun." My shoulders are beginning to unglue from my ears
when I realize I'm being watched.

An old man—seated, pin-striped suit, briefcase clenched
in his lap—stares up at me, practically licking his lips. My
heart chokes. Was he back there, at the club? Did he see me
take off my bra? Or does he just know what I am, because he's
one of them? They all know, the pedophiles. They can smell
us our whole lives, not only when we're young. Like hunting
dogs smell rabbits, and we smell them.

Run.

Head down, I push my way—"Sorry, sorry, sorry"—to the front of the car, near the conductor's metal booth. I'm better here, with the old man out of sight. A seat opens up, and I drop into it, turning toward the black window.

If you love yourself so much, why don't you marry yourself? my sister used to tease. But that's not why I'm pulled to my reflection. I'm not admiring myself; I'm judging, dissecting, wishing the person looking back at me would be someone different. Someone better.

This is exactly what I'm wishing when the Q climbs above ground and my same-old face vanishes, replaced by the flashing girders of the Manhattan Bridge, ferries gliding on the water, and the new downtown skyscape with its twin beams of light where the World Trade Center stood, a few long months ago. Even with the old man in pinstripes not fifty feet away, I'm swept up by that view.

She's out there, my someone better. She's got to be.

11

SOMEBODY.
ANYBODY.
HELP ME!

2002

Twenty-five years old

My roommates and I have been Blockbuster-binging female action thrillers—Geena Davis in *The Long Kiss Goodnight*, Angelina Jolie in *Lara Croft: Tomb Raider*, Pam Grier in *Jackie Brown*. Watching women defy the rules and refuse to be used makes my arm hairs stand up. It makes me want to fight back, too.

I'd better, or else.

I seem to have opened a portal, that day at the strip club. Lately, no matter where I go or what I'm doing, he finds me, reaches his bony hand up from hell and tries to drag me back.

Fighting a demon in your mind doesn't feel badass or he-
roic, it feels pointless and pathetic. But not all life-or-death
battles are big box office thrillers populated by A-list actors.
If my story were a movie, it would be an indie short, a quiet
dark comedy starring a nobody—me—because that's all I can
afford.

...

ACT ONE

INT. BATHROOM — DAY

KIMBERLY (mid-twenties) is wedged into the space
between the toilet and the wall. Strewn across
the bathmat are the contents of her dance bag:
toe shoes, makeup, a curling iron, etc. From
beyond the bathroom, we hear SERGE and NATASHA,
Kimberly's roommates, watching an action movie.

                    SERGE (O.S.)
          Twiggy, get in here! Angelina's slaying!

                    KIMBERLY
                 (between sobs)
          Go ahead without me!

Kimberly struggles to dial the cordless phone in
her trembling hands.

                    WOMAN (V.O.)
          Information, what number please?

                    KIMBERLY
                 (whispering)
          Yes, can I please have the number for
          the RAINN hotline?

INTERCUT — PHONE CONVERSATION

                    MAN
          Good afternoon, this is Rain, may I help
          you?

Kimberly bursts into tears.

                    MAN
          Hello?

                    KIMBERLY
          Sorry, hi, I think I might be losing
          my mind? I was just walking down the
          street and passed this man wearing Old
          Spice and I almost didn't make it home—

Explosions, gunfire, screaming, from the living
room TV.

                    MAN
          Ma'am? Ma'am? What's happening?

                    KIMBERLY
              (wipes her nose on her knees)
          Sorry, my roommates are watching a
          movie. I forgot to say I was . . .
          molested. And I think I need real
          help. I'm not going to kill myself or
          anything, at least I don't think—

                    MAN
          Excuse me, ma'am?

                    KIMBERLY
          Please! Will you just let me talk?

She takes a deep breath.

                    KIMBERLY (CONT'D)
          Thank you so much. Also, I'm seeing
          things, in my flashbacks, that I never
          saw before, and I don't know if they're
          real?

No response.

                    KIMBERLY (CONT'D)
          Sir?

                    MAN
          Ma'am, this is a Thai restaurant.

                    KIMBERLY
                    (quietly half-sobbing, half-
                    laughing)

                    MAN
          I'm so very, very sorry for what
          happened to you.

                    KIMBERLY
                    (breathing easier now)
          Thanks.

The panic attack has blown over, along with Kimberly's urgent need to call RAINN—the Rape, Abuse
& Incest National Network. But it's obviously time
to figure some shit out.

                    ACT TWO

EXT. WEST VILLAGE CHURCH — SUNSET

Kimberly, just off a bar mitzvah shift, strides
along a busy sidewalk. Checking her watch, she
winces, walks faster. Outside a Unitarian church
with both an American flag and an LGBTQ rainbow
flag flying over its doors, she checks a flyer in her
hand . . .

INSERT — THE FLYER

                SIA Meetings
        Survivors of Incest Anonymous
  for adult survivors of childhood sexual abuse.

BACK TO SCENE

A gust of wind blows the flyer from Kimberly's
hand.

INSERT — FLIP-SIDE OF AIRBORNE FLYER

 Names and identifying details have been changed
 to honor the privacy of 12-Step group members.

INT. CHURCH STAIRCASE — EVENING

Kimberly runs, sideways-looking-over-her-
shoulder, up a staircase to the second floor, where
multiple meeting rooms flank a fluorescent-lit hallway.
Kimberly beelines for the first open door.

INT. CHURCH MEETING ROOM — EVENING

Eight people of varying ages sit in a circle on
folding chairs. A BUSINESSMAN in a suit and tie
has the floor. Seeing Kimberly at the door, he
pauses. All eyes turn to Kimberly.

                    KIMBERLY
          Sorry, so sorry I'm late!

The GROUP LEADER (forties) handsome, clean-cut,
smiles, gesturing to an open chair. Kimberly
slinks into the seat, scoping out the room. She's
one of only two women in it.

                    BUSINESSMAN
          So, it's just been a merry-go-round,
          you know? The coke leads to the
          acting-out leads to the coke leads
          to the acting-out. Until I get clean,
          there's probably no point in me coming
          here, frankly.

Kimberly looks uneasy.

                    GROUP LEADER
          Thank you, Dan.

The Group Leader gestures to the man directly to
Kimberly's left.

                        GROUP LEADER (CONT'D)
          Michael?

                            MICHAEL
          My name is Michael, and I'm intimacy
          avoidant . . .

As Michael speaks about his struggles with porn-
ography, Kimberly fidgets in her chair. When his
monologue ends, the Group Leader motions to her.

                         GROUP LEADER
          Hi. Welcome to our meeting. We know the
          courage it takes to walk into these
          rooms for the first time. Would you like
          to tell us a little bit about yourself?

                            KIMBERLY
          I'm so sorry, but what is this meeting,
          actually?

                         GROUP LEADER
          This is SAA, Sex Addicts Anonymous.

                            KIMBERLY
          Oh! I'm not supposed to be here. I
          apologize.

She reaches for her bag.

                         GROUP LEADER
          No need to apologize. You don't have to
          talk or make excuses. Why don't we skip
          you for this week, and if you feel like
          talking next week you can?

Kimberly opens her mouth, then takes in the circle
of sympathetic faces around her.

                            KIMBERLY
          That sounds nice, thank you.

For the next forty minutes, Kimberly listens to
the others' testimonies about sexual addiction.

As the meeting draws to a close, she joins hands
with the circle and bows her head as they recite a
prayer.

                    THE GROUP
              God, grant me the serenity
              To accept the things I cannot change,
              The courage to change the things I can,
              And the wisdom to know the difference.

Kimberly breaks free before the prayer ends,
bolting down the hall, past a closed door taped
with a small sign: SIA, Welcome!

MINUTES LATER

INT. CHAPEL — EVENING

Kimberly is seated in a pew in the empty chapel
below the meeting rooms, glaring up at a plain white
cross.

                    KIMBERLY
              (under her breath, to God)
          Clearly, this is funny to you.

                   ACT THREE

EXT. NEW YORK STATE THRUWAY — DAY

It's stop-and-go traffic, rush hour.

INT. KIMBERLY'S HONDA — DAY

Kimberly, bawling so ferociously that other drivers
turn and gawk, blasts "Silent All These Years" by
Tori Amos.

ONE HOUR LATER

INT. KIMBERLY'S HONDA, COUNTRY ROAD — EVENING
Kimberly slams to a stop.

                    KIMBERLY
              I can't do this!

She makes a U-turn, speeds angrily back toward the freeway.

FLASHBACK

Aunt Pat cross-legged in her studio: "Do not avoid your suffering. Feel it and let it go!"

END FLASHBACK

>   KIMBERLY
>   (to herself)
>   Yes you can.

She veers the Honda around again, pulling into a mostly empty parking lot outside a quaint white-shingled community center. Women begin to trickle into the building. GRACE, a twentysomething in badass thigh-high boots, holds the door for GOLDIE, a regal seventysomething who walks with a cane. Kimberly cleans herself up in the rear-view.

>   KIMBERLY
>   (to self in mirror)
>   To thrive or merely exist? That's the
>   question.

MINUTES LATER

INT — CONNECTICUT COMMUNITY CENTER — EVENING

A dozen or so women—of all ages, from all walks of life—drink coffee and eat cookies. Kimberly crosses the room to take a seat. At precisely 7:00 PM, Goldie taps a microphone on a podium.

>   GOLDIE
>   My name is Goldie, and I will be
>   facilitating this six-week session of
>   Survivors of Incest Anonymous. Welcome!

Goldie pauses to look around the room, meeting eyes with each of the women, then begins reading from the SIA LEADERS GUIDE . . .

                    GOLDIE (CONT'D)
          We are a closed 12-Step program for
          women who have experienced incest, which
          we define broadly as a sexual encounter
          by a family member or extended family
          member that damaged the child. SIA is
          not a replacement for therapy . . .

Kimberly frowns, raking her thighs with her finger-
nails.

                    GOLDIE (CONT'D)
          . . . but it *is* a place to experience
          hope, camaraderie, and recovery.

Kimberly stops raking.

                                        DISSOLVE TO:

MONTAGE — THE NEXT SEVERAL WEEKS

INT. CONNECTICUT COMMUNITY CENTER — EVENING

Kimberly listens in awe as Grace, in a different
pair of badass boots, wraps up a story. Goldie
gestures to Kimberly: Would she like to speak?
Kimberly shakes her head.

                    GOLDIE (V.O.)
          We learn in SIA not to deny; that we did
          not imagine the abuse, nor was it our
          fault in any way.

INT. KIMBERLY'S APARTMENT — DAY

Kimberly steps on her scale, nodding at the low,
low number.

                    GOLDIE (V.O.)
          We had healthy, natural needs for love,
          attention, and acceptance, and we often
          paid high prices to get those needs met.

EXT. OCEANSIDE BOAT YARD — DAY

Kimberly helps her DAD wash his boat. They work side by side in unison, not speaking.

> GOLDIE (V.O.)
> We felt we had to protect our nonabusive caretakers from this horrible secret, as if they were not participants. Our feelings of betrayal are immeasurable.

INT. BROOKLYN STORAGE UNIT — NIGHT

Kimberly opens a battered moving box containing her porcelain dolls from childhood. She regards it awhile, then closes it up and labels it GOOD WILL.

> GOLDIE (V.O.)
> We need to mourn the death of the ideal family that many of us created in our own imaginations.

INT. CONNECTICUT COMMUNITY CENTER — EVENING

Once again, Goldie gestures to Kimberly: Would she like to speak? This time, Kimberly nods, and the group leans in.

> GOLDIE (V.O.)
> We will never forget, but we can, in time, end the regret.

ONE HOUR LATER

EXT. CONNECTICUT COMMUNITY CENTER PARKING LOT — EVENING

Kimberly walks outside, flanked by the others.

> GOLDIE (V.O.)
> In dealing with this pain, it feels like we are pulling the scab off a wound that never healed properly—and it hurts! However, it's easier to cry when we have friends who are not afraid of

our tears. We can be comforted—that's
why we're here.

At Grace's urging, Kimberly retrieves from her car
a brand-new comp card, which the women pass around
and admire.

INSERT — THE COMP CARD

An amateurish collage of pixelated photos of Kimberly breakdancing in mismatched shoes, with text:

Kimberly Shannon, Dancer/Model

EXT. CLEAR TALENT GROUP HEADQUARTERS, NEW YORK
CITY — DAY

Kimberly stands on a crowded sidewalk in her dance
gear, looking up.

> GOLDIE (V.O.)
> We have come to the awesome realization
> that our pain is temporary, but denial
> and its consequences are forever. And if
> any one of us can recover, then so can
> we all.

Kimberly reaches into her dance bag for a handful
of her comp cards and, bracing, heads inside.

FADE TO BLACK

12

HUNG BY
A SILK

2003
Twenty-six years old

Commercials are where the money is, not backup dancing. But you can't get an audition without an agent and you can't get an agent without experience and you can't get a job unless you're in the Screen Actors Guild and you can't get into SAG unless you have a job and you can't get a job without an audition, which you can't get without an agent. . . .

That's what I know, and where I'm trapped, a tiny fly in a great big web. But I refuse to die here. Of all the ways to go, I won't go stuck.

I don't mean to complain. I've been teaching dance to little kids, which is . . . bittersweet. When I send them *grand jeté*-ing across the floor, I can't help but see her, my little-girl self, leaping with them. Released from her secret cage, she is beautiful and complete—free, if only for the moment.

When I'm not teaching a class or working a bar mitzvah, I return to the Clear Talent Group offices to stalk Jaime, the head of the choreography and dance department. Some days, the receptionist asks me to leave, but others, she lets me wait in the lobby, where I make sure to sit in the sight line of Jaime's glass-walled office. Last week, I managed to catch his eye. He popped his head out and stuck out his hand, and I rushed over to shake it, handing him another comp card. I'd left one for him the week before, but my goal was to hand one to him personally. "I appreciate how hard you're trying here," he said, before telling me to come back when I had more experience. I came back the next day, one day more experienced.

All I need is for someone to give me a chance.

...

"Kimberly Shannon, with the mismatched shoes?" says the voice on the other end of my new Nokia cell phone. (I got it from Timmy's friend at the Verizon store because you have to have a phone to work now. Timmy still looks out for me, even if he doesn't want me.)

"That's me!"

"I just *loved* your card," the voice says. "Let's meet!"

"I can come right now!" I say. "Who is this?"

———

Chris Harrison is a wiry, kooky guy in his thirties with a super-white smile that never ebbs. In his jumbled office, surrounded by photographs of his Cirque du Soleil–style troupe, AntiGravity, I tell him I've recently left the Ailey School to pursue my career—omitting the part about the car accident and getting dropped. He doesn't need to know that I'm still healing, that my brain isn't speaking fluently to my legs. He might not care, anyway. Apparently, the mismatched shoes in my comp card photos (a choice that my friends tried to talk me out of) have told him what he needs to know about me.

"We have a show coming up in Central Park next week," he says, after five minutes of chitchat. "I want to end with a dance number. How about you help create it?"

"Really?" I say, a mixed shot of adrenaline and panic slicing through me. "With AntiGravity? Next week?"

"If you don't think you can handle it . . ." Chris shrugs, still smiling, baiting me. How does this total stranger know me so well?

Flash cut to a stage under the trees in Central Park, where I'm performing with a dozen of the world's most incredible gymnasts and acrobats. I'm way out of my league, but it doesn't trip me up like at the Ailey School. As I learned in SIA, when you come from a family that's stuck in the dark, you need to look elsewhere for guiding lights. These exceptional performers don't have to be my competition; they can be my inspiration.

Soon, I have my second opportunity to show Chris he made the right bet. AntiGravity is doing a photo shoot with *FHM* magazine, and he's asked me to be a part of it. This could be the biggest opportunity of my lifetime. So what if we're going to be suspended from the ceiling on silk ropes and I've never done aerial work? If someone believes in you, against all odds, what kind of person would you be not to at least *try*? Exactly, a rude person.

An hour before the shoot I try to take a shower but I can't move, can't seem to lift my foot off the bath mat and step over the shower ledge. If not for my greasy hair, I'd skip it—like I have all week, which is why the hair problem. But I won't show up to a photo shoot for *FHM*, a real magazine with celebrities and perfume ads, looking like a mangy cat. I pick up my foot. I get in.

At first the hot soapy water washing down my body feels good. Then it starts—the shrinking. "*Please, please, not today.*" I hold the wall, try to stay tall and present, but my hands slip down the tiles. I'm eleven, I'm ten, I'm nine, I'm eight.

He steps in.

Grabbing my shoulders, he yanks my chin upward, jams his hard thing against my sputtering, sealed lips.

"Open your mouth," he says, water raining down.

I wrap my skinny arms around myself, shaking my head.

"Open your mouth," he repeats.

I pull away, curling tighter, eyes on my red-painted toes. Mom takes such good care of my toes.

He grips my jaw: "I'll have to open it for you, then."

When the flashback spits me out, choking, I'm still my little-girl self—pressed so hard against the cold tiles that with luck they'll collapse and suck me in. I can still hear the echo of him, telling me what to do. But the tiles are white, not blue.

Reaching up, I feel for my watch on the shower ledge. It's 8:17 AM. I'd have to leave right this second to get to Milk Studios on time. There's no way, absolutely no way.

Until I think of Grace.

Grace, with the warrior boots, from SIA. Grace, who checked out law books from the library, got emancipated from her parents when she turned fifteen, found a lawyer, and took her molester dad to court.

"Don't be such a baby," I say, lifting myself up. "Grace put her dad in jail. You can get out of the fucking shower."

...

I didn't know it was a lingerie shoot, but that's okay! No problem at all! It's also totally fine that I have no idea how I'm going to pull this off. After the Central Park show, I asked some of the AntiGravity girls if they'd show me how to do aerial silks—what we're doing today for *FHM*—and just like that, everyone vanished from the studio. Ever since I showed up at

AntiGravity, I've felt a coolness from the other performers. This will change, once I've proven myself, but not yet. There's not a lot of work for aerialists, and for now, I'm just some random breakdancer girl who Chris took a shine to. Everyone is protecting their job. I get it. I'll figure it out.

The photographer says he wants a shot of all four of us "stars" hanging upside down in a cluster. The real pros, Alex (two-time Slovakian rhythmic gymnastics champion), Katya (six-year veteran of Russia's national gymnastics team), and Caroline (one of the company's top performers) are already in position, casually chatting and stretching on white silks suspended from the rafters. About ten people I don't recognize, plus two guys from AntiGravity who must've come to assist (*they're* not wearing only underwear anyway), are nice enough. But the aerialists—in red lingerie, too—seem not to notice me. I wave up to them. *See how friendly and noncompetitive I am?* But the girls are in their own world. How do I get up there? Obviously, I can't ask, and everyone's waiting.

I grab the last pair of dangling silks as a single rope and start hiking myself up, one hand in front of the other. Nearing the top, I note the others have knotted their silks around one foot, creating an anchor. I reach down to do the same, but this sends me spinning, the ends of my silks twirling loose. I straighten my legs, swinging like a monkey on a vine.

"Someone help her with her foot lock!" Alex calls, as I ricochet off her bare thigh.

Just when I think I can't hang on another second, one of the AntiGravity guys comes to my rescue, knotting the fabric around the arch of my right foot.

"All right now?" yells the photographer, pointing his camera up.

"Yes, fine, thanks!" I squeak, shaking the blood back into my numb, rope-burned hand. "So sorry about that, Alex!"

She doesn't seem to hear me.

The photographer's shutter starts clicking. "Just do what you do, ladies!"

For the others, this is a logical directive. They can just do what they do because they actually do this. Last year, while I was performing for thirteen-year-olds at bar mitzvahs, Alex, Katya, and Caroline were performing with No Doubt at the Grammys. I try copying their graceful twirls and flips, but my silks keep tangling up, and soon the AntiGravity guy appears to rescue me again.

"Lower down a bit, below the others. Good, now try the splits? I'll hold you."

For the next few minutes, I hang there with his hand on my butt while the girls whirl above, together but separate, like pieces on a mobile.

Eventually, someone calls for a break and we shimmy down, to applause (not for me, obviously) from the crew. My satin bustier is dappled with sweat, and my legs are shaking, but I did it. I showed up and tried, at least. All I want to do now is put on my sweats, but the other three aren't covering up, so I don't, either.

The girls stand by the windows, devouring tea sandwiches and waving down to people on the sidewalks. They wear lingerie the way I used to wear my cheerleading skirt—like armor. But their confidence isn't an act, the way mine was.

Look at them! They're perfect. I lean deeper into my corner by the clothing racks, holding my grumbling stomach.

The bossy stylist approaches the girls, showing them a clothes hanger draped with a pink-and-black lace bra and a loop of black string. "We need a thong in the mix," she says. "Which one of you wants to rock this?" The girls pinch the thong like it has cooties, wrinkle their noses, shake their heads.

"I think the fabric part is missing?" jokes Alex. "It's literally just a string!"

She's only half right. From way over here, I can see the string is not *just* a string, it's a line to cross: the line between sexy and pornographic, empowering and humiliating. It's not just underwear, it's pornwear. Posing in it would be as good as posing naked. Alex, Katya, and Caroline are at the top of their game, the best of the best. What could they possibly gain by saying yes?

Her best options ruled out, the stylist clacks over to my corner and thrusts her hanger at me. "If you could go ahead and put this on," she says, like it's a done deal, "we're shooting in ten."

"Um . . ." Nausea ripples through me.

Fifteen minutes later, I'm back on set, hiding the so-called thong and the lacy bra under a silk robe. The room is tilting, the way unsafe places do. *Just get through it.* I walk straight toward the lights. No one can know that I'm having a panic attack, that I just threw up in the bathroom, that I hate this thing they've put me into.

This time, the photographer doesn't ask me to perform. He knows what he's dealing with, keeps it simple. "Just lift your knee, arch your back, and stay very still," he instructs.

I'll do it. I'll be a body, a statue, a pleasing arrangement. But this, I tell myself, is the last time.

...

When the March 2004 issue of *FHM* comes out, the first person I call, the first person I want to show that I'm going places, is Dad: "Go buy the new issue of *FHM*. Go right now, okay?"

Twenty minutes later, he calls me back, confused: "Why are you on the cover? I can't believe you're on the cover!"

"No, Dad, that's Paris Hilton! Turn to page thirty-six."

Pages ruffle in the background. He clears his throat.

"Dad?"

"Well, I'll be darned," he says. "That's you?"

"Yep, the full-page one, and the inset," I say. The inset, a two-inch image of us suspended in a tight cluster, is tucked into the article's text, under a giant picture of me, arching backward, one knee bent, as instructed, in the pornwear.

There's another silence while Dad probably lights a cigarette. He starts to read the article out loud: "'Kimberly Shannon Murphy, from . . .' Aw, for Pete's sake, they say you're from Ocean City!"

"It doesn't matter, Dad."

He takes a long puff, continuing: "'. . . from Ocean City,

New York, is trained in modern ballet and breakdancing. *Guys will ask if I can put my ankles behind my head*, she says.' Aw, Kim, that's—"

"Shut up and keep reading!" I demand. "Read the part about the limo."

I imagine him squinting as he scans the text for the part about the limo. "Aha!" he says. "Here it is: *I've broken my legs three times, but that was doing other things. I got run over by a limo at my prom. My date didn't go to the hospital with me, but my dad did.*' Well, whaddya know? The old Dad gets some credit, finally."

I laugh. "I thought you'd like that."

We both know that's not how it went. I begged to go to the hospital that night, but Dad took me home, instead. "It's four AM, are you nuts?" he'd said, as I writhed in the passenger seat. "Your leg looks fine to me." It was Mom who took me, the next day. Only when she brought me home in a cast did Dad believe my leg was broken (in five places, as a matter of fact).

I didn't intentionally mislead the magazine writer. I just told the story I wanted to believe. Sometimes it's okay to do that. Sometimes you *have* to do that, just to survive.

13

THE JUMP

2004

Twenty-seven years old

All those years of barely scraping by, of running between odd jobs, of wanting more but feeling unworthy: let them be behind me. I have not one but *two* agents looking out for me now.

So I don't regret the lingerie shoot. That picture changed my life. The magazine was still on newsstands when I got the Old Navy commercial. It all happened so fast:

One minute I was holding my dog-eared copy of *FHM* in an agent's face, saying, "Look, I'm in a magazine! *Now* will you send me out for auditions?"

The next minute—poof!—there I was, breakdancing on a yacht in Florida, a makeup assistant shading me with a parasol between takes.

That's what it felt like, anyway, in spite of the two weeks

of auditions and callbacks it took to get the job. The other girls on the yacht, including the commercial's star, warned me it would probably never air, so I shouldn't expect to make residuals. But it did air. They aired the heck out of that commercial, and I earned forty grand—just enough to pay off all my credit card and student debt.

A few months later, I was working a bar mitzvah, and a kid came up to me: "Are you the Old Navy girl?"

I said yes.

His mouth dropped; he shook his shaggy head. "What are you doing *here*?"

"Good question!" I said. And that was my last bar mitzvah.

I still pound the pavement seven days a week, only now I'm running from audition to audition and airport to airport, traveling to perform with AntiGravity. I've worked in Italy, Spain, Morocco, Panama, El Salvador, and all over the United States. The idea of going back to my old life, calling Timmy when I can't make my rent or pay my medical bills, is unfathomable, so I don't stop. Ever.

One day, about six months after shooting the Old Navy commercial, I'm standing on a sidewalk, in line for an "audition" to be paid two hundred dollars to dye my hair for a TV commercial, when my Nokia rings. It's George Aguilar, only *the* most famous stunt coordinator in New York. Some of my friends from AntiGravity are starting to get into stunt work, and they encouraged me to send George my comp card. A shot in the dark, I figured.

"I want to see you about doubling Uma Thurman," George says. "Can you meet me right now?"

On the inside, I faint like a Victorian lady in a too-tight corset. But on the outside, I act. I break free of that line and run for a taxi—I can afford a taxi! Minutes later, I'm in George's office, shaking his hand. Framed in the window behind him, right across the street, is Club Shelter—a good omen.

George puts me immediately, strangely, at ease. Handsome and soft-spoken, he could be anywhere from twenty to fifty—I truly can't tell. The man is ageless—maybe an angel? His calm, steady way reminds me of Aunt Pat.

"Are you"—he squints at the top of my head—"five-nine?"

"And a quarter," I say.

"Hmm," he says. "Uma's about six feet."

It just so happens that I have a pair of high heels in my messenger bag, for occasions like this. I rip off my sneakers and step into them.

"Now I am, too," I say.

George laughs. "Do you have your book with you?"

I whip it out of my bag.

"The movie is called *My Super Ex-Girlfriend*," says George. "I think you should meet the director." He says it will mean an entire *year* of full-time work—a whole year of safety.

He takes me to meet the director, Ivan Reitman, who is not ageless (to my eye, he's seriously ancient) and does not put me at ease.

"George tells me you've never done a movie before!" Ivan says, looking me up and down.

"No."

"Well"—he holds out a trembly hand—"let me see your book, then." I quickly hand it over before he can snap his fingers at me.

He turns the pages, frowning. "We'd have to put a wig on you. You've *never* done stunts?"

I shake my head. "Not for the movies. But I do aerial work and breakdancing. I performed for the king of Morocco, at his palace!"

This is true, if apparently uninteresting to Ivan. Still, he seems to smell my hunger and think it can work in his favor. He gives me a shot but says I need Uma's approval to get the job.

First, I have to learn . . . everything. Uma's character in the movie, G-Girl, fights all her battles in the air, so for the next two weeks, George works with me on the wire. Thanks to the harness work I've done with AntiGravity, the stunts come easily. When George finds out I can do flips, he loses his mind. "Where have you been for the last ten years?" he whoops. The stunt world is dominated by former gymnasts, who tend to be petite, not tall, which makes me a rarity; the extra inches that worked against me in high school gymnastics are now my secret weapon, making me the best option George has found to double his willowy star. That doesn't mean I'll sleep well until she approves me. I'm not eating much, either. Uma's as thin as a reed, and I need to look like her.

I'm upside down on a wire the first time we meet.

"Hi there!" She waves up to me. She is absolutely breathtaking. How does she light up the whole room like that?

"Show her what you can do!" George says.

I move through a sequence of flips before signaling the rigger to lower me down. I curtsy a little as I shake Uma's hand, and it takes all my power to briefly meet her blindingly blue gaze. This isn't just any star, this is Mia Wallace from *Pulp Fiction*, the Bride from *Kill Bill*. When I look at Uma, I see a woman who knows her worth. I also see a woman who holds my future in her hands.

"Can I have a go?" she asks.

This throws me for a loop. I know it's the double's job to outfit her actor in a harness and guide her through the easier stunts, but George is still teaching me all of this. I'm not ready to teach someone else! I look to George, who wants me to succeed nearly as much as I want to. If I don't, he'll have to start the process all over with someone new. "Go ahead," he says with a nod. Willing my hands not to shake, I put Uma in the harness—attaching her wires, tightening the shackles, counting the two clicks like the riggers taught me. Seeing how nervous I am, they step in to coach her through some easy flying moves.

A half hour later, Uma glides from the room, taking her light with her. "Kimberly will be great!" she calls back to George. "I'll send her to my guy for extensions."

Uma's guy is Ryan Trygstad at Sally Hershberger—just about the fanciest salon in the city. He opens up the place just for me, sits me in a plush chair before a mirror framed by orchid plants.

"Cappuccino?" he asks, squeezing my arm. "Champagne?"

"Just water, thank you." You never know how much a drink will cost you in New York City, and I'm already sick to my stomach thinking about how much the extensions will set me back. Whatever! I've already decided it's worth it. I'll sell my car, if that's what it takes.

Five hours later, I have thick, luscious hair for the first time in my life. As Ryan loads me up with special shampoos and conditioners and brushes, I get the nerve to ask how much it all costs.

"Oh, no!" he laughs. "You don't owe me anything. They're paying *you* to be here."

I call George to see if there's been a mistake. The last thing I need is to get fired over "free" hair extensions that aren't free. Nothing is *ever* free. And what did Ryan mean about my getting paid to have my hair done?

"We started shooting last week," George explains. "And as long as we're shooting this film, you're getting paid."

"But I haven't even been on set," I say. "I don't understand."

"You're on hold. We need you to be available at a moment's notice, so we're paying you not to take other work," says George. "We'll need you in about a month. Till then, you're good!"

Weeks go by. The checks keep coming. The number on the scale keeps falling. Still no call from George. I show up on set: "Can I at least move some mats around or something?" He tells me that won't be necessary. "Just enjoy your free time." As if. The very idea of "free time" makes me want to jump out of my skin. Only Dad would understand where I'm at right now. "I didn't join the Marine Corps to sit in a parking lot and pick up cigarette butts," he always says. I miss him; we haven't been talking, lately. Since going to SIA, I bring up the past too much for his liking, and I refuse to stuff it back down.

One day, to kill time, I go to Starbucks and "relax" at a corner table with my back to the wall, looking out for whoever will be coming to remove the hair extensions and make me give back the money they've paid me so far—the money I won't believe is mine until they let me earn it. That's where I am when George finally calls: "Good news: you start Monday!"

I jump to my feet. "Really?"

"You'll be hitting a breakaway table, so make sure your stunt bag's stocked with a back pad and whatever else you might need."

"Yep, no problem!" I say.

I call a friend who's in the business. "What's a stunt bag, and what's a back pad, and where do I get them?" I'm too embarrassed to ask what a breakaway table is, and how I'm supposed to break it. We didn't practice that in rehearsals.

My friend directs me to *the* stunt website, where I put in a rush order for the bag and everything to go in it. The stuff arrives just in time for my first day of shooting, for which I arrive an hour and forty-five minutes early, making sure to tell everyone it's my first day ever so they'll forgive me for all the mistakes I'm about to make.

In Hair and Makeup, they put a brown wig on me to match

G-Girl's mousy alter ego, Jenny. I strap on my new body pads and waddle up to George, looking more like the Michelin Man than a superheroine. George is too kind and polite to laugh, but I can see how hard he's trying not to. Confirmed: I've gone too far with the padding. I rip most of it off and follow my boss to the middle of a closed-off Upper East Side block swarming with extras, stuntpeople, and cameramen. I already love this world within a world. There are rules, here, and the dangers are mine to choose.

George points to a springboard attached to a four-foot-high platform on the sidewalk. "You'll jump off that, make a half turn, and land there." He points to a street vendor's table piled high with handbags. "You'll have to get some air to make it. And be sure to land in the middle to trigger the breakaway. The bags will soften your fall."

"No problem," I say, my nervousness shifting into excitement. I've jumped off springboards like that thousands of times for gymnastics. That part's going to be easy. The landing I'm less confident about. But I can't wait to do this stunt. Never in my life, other than some nights at Club Shelter, have I felt like this: I'm exactly where I'm meant to be.

It's time. The stunt crew eyes me as I stand for "last looks," the final touch-ups to hair, makeup, and wardrobe before the cameras roll. Now I'm back to nervous again. How many takes will I need? Will I fold under the pressure? Miss my mark and embarrass myself in front of the whole set? I'm already learning it's true what they say about women having to work twice as hard to be taken seriously in this business. The New York stunt world is especially tough. Rumor has it, some of the East Coast guys were in the Mafia before they became stuntmen. I believe it.

One of the men, an ND, or nondescript—that's like a supporting actor to the main stuntperson in a stunt scene, where it's not safe for regular actors to be—paces up to the edge of my platform as I'm waiting for my cue.

"Hey, gymnast!" he barks up at me. "This isn't a fucking gymnastics meet. We're not going to score you, so no pretty landings, got it?"

Just like that, my butterflies vanish. This guy doesn't know my dad.

Go ahead and doubt me.

"Three, two, one, action!" calls the director.

The jump symbolizes everything, and I nail it.

Part III

LANDING

14

GOOD
THERAPY

2007

Thirty years old

It turns out every stunt is symbolic, a new declaration that
I'm in control of my life, goddammit, no one else. So as long as I
hit my mark, I don't mind getting a little scratched up. Pain
is part of the deal, why fight it? Sometimes I hope for it. A
double on the last film I worked on got taken away in an ambulance, and I was jealous. I have not yet grasped how completely fucked up that is.

At the moment, I'm relaxing on my gurney in a crowded,
quite frankly filthy, Brooklyn ER. I've had a little fall on the
set of *I Am Legend.* Fine, a big fall. Those poor riggers. They
felt so bad. Shit happens in this business. There are systems,
checklists, and coordinators to protect us, but they sometimes
fail—and everyone gets very upset if they do.

I love my job because I understand it. It's all right out in the open. Even the stunt guys, as tough as they are, make sense to me. Let's face it, we're all missing a chip. Lots of us have been through things. I don't think anyone with a fully sane brain would wake up on a Monday morning and say, *Let's go do a car hit*. Or, in my case, *Let's go face-first through a second-story window.*

Please hurry up and take care of me, Doctor. I told the transpo guy who brought me here not to leave without me. I need to get back.

The surgeon finally comes at 6:00 PM. He's cute, whatever he looks like. The white coat and clipboard are all I need to see, the whole fantasy. He hasn't even looked at me yet, and already I feel better.

But there's a curtain on a track, kind of like a shower curtain, next to my gurney, and the doctor is starting to pull it closed around us.

"Please leave that!" I snap, jerking upright.

He stops, takes me in, quickly recovers. "No problem," he says, and I relax, trusting him—too easily, it will turn out.

The surgeon washes up, then begins peeling off the soaked bandages the first ER doctor applied. "At what time, exactly, did this happen?"

"Nine thirty," I say.

The doctor's lips tighten. "Ideally, I'd have gotten to you sooner."

He peers at the slit running from under my right eye down to my lip, "This, I'll glue. But your lip needs stitches. A lot of them. There could be scarring."

I figured. Everyone kept yelling at me, *Get to the ER before you scar up*, but I refused. My fall had set production back, and I wasn't about to leave them in the lurch. Or God forbid, get replaced. I was picked for the window jump out of all the "creatures," and it was my first time working with the guys from LA, the best guys in the world. I needed them to see me succeed. So I doused my face with hydrogen peroxide and stayed for three more takes.

"Will I have to go under?" I ask the doctor, hopefully.

Sadly, I will not. I like going under. The peacefulness of counting down from ten, of never reaching one. The comforting moment between there and not-there. If that was the last feeling I ever felt, I'd be okay with it.

But I always wake up—to the same reality. Which, these days, from an outsider's point of view, probably looks like a nice one. It helps to remember that. If only I could see myself the same way: in the present tense.

The surgeon injects my face with several shots of novocaine, and gets to work right there at my gurney. I brace against the numb tugging at my lip and make polite *hmm*-ing sounds as he tells me that his real office is on Park Avenue, but he volunteers here once a week to help people in need. The way he says "people in need," I know he's talking about patients with no insurance, the poor, the homeless. That's not me anymore. I need him in a different way, though.

"Do you do *boobth*?" I lisp, through my cotton wads, as soon as he finishes.

He gives me a look. "Yes, I do."

———

After convincing the transpo guy to take me back to the warehouse, I melt into the back seat of the van, twirling the surgeon's card between my bandaged fingers. When he asked why I wanted implants, I said I was tired of looking like a boy. But that wasn't exactly true. What I'm tired of is looking like a helpless little girl.

...

Three months later

When I wake up after my breast surgery, there are two large half cantaloupes attached to my chest. "Are these Bs?" I ask the doctor, feeling dizzy. "I said Bs!"

"Everybody says that," he answers, no longer so cute. "Then they come back: '*Doc, make them bigger.*' I thought I'd save you the trouble."

"Oh," I say. I'm about to thank him—he's a doctor, after all—but I stop myself. At least I can say I stop myself.

...

For my birthday, Grandma Gen sent me the usual check inside a card that said YOU ARE MORE PRECIOUS THAN GEMSTONES! with foil jewels on the front. "Dear Kimberly," read the note, "I'm so proud of the successful woman you've become. I hope you can be happy now." I placed the check back inside the card, slid the card into the purple envelope, and ripped them in half, in half again, then into itty-bitty birthday confetti over the garbage can.

I don't need her money anymore.

Since George gave me my break with *My Super Ex-Girlfriend*, I've worked nonstop on movies like *Spider-Man 3*, *Across the Universe*, and *Enchanted*; and on TV shows like *Ugly Betty*, *Gossip Girl*, and *Rescue Me*. My career is going so well that I've bought an apartment in Williamsburg.

Now I'm on my way to my first appointment with a fancy therapist on the Upper West Side. Her name is Andrea, and she's the real deal, according to her address and price tag.

Not that I *want* to go. I'm dreading it, now that the day has come. I get off the train twenty blocks away from Andrea's office, house music playing on my new iPod. I was hoping to walk off my nerves, but they're just getting worse by the block. What are the chances Andrea will be better than every other therapist I've tried?

I think of the first one, Mom's, badgering me to cough up the details of my abuse, only hours after I'd remembered it in the first place. I was just a kid! Why couldn't anyone see that?

I think of the sweet woman in her seventies who met with me in her cluttered apartment for free when I had no money. She was so kind, I forgave her for falling asleep during every one of our sessions. Still, it was only slightly more productive than talking to an empty chair.

And then there was that sliding-scale shrink I saw a single time in my twenties. I can hear her response to my life story like it was a second ago: "Oh honey," she said, "do you know how many women like you are shooting heroin on a street corner? You should feel proud just to be alive!" That's when I walked out.

Fuck that lady and her low bar. I wish I could remember her name so I could write her a letter: *"Just in case you come across another person like me, please give them better advice. . . ."*

...

Andrea's waiting room is the nicest I've ever been in. It's bright and sunny, with pastel walls, big comfy armchairs, and shelves decorated with geodes and pottery from around the world—like a more polished version of Aunt Pat's bodywork studio. When Andrea comes out to greet me, I feel even more at home.

Standing eye to eye with me in flats, jeans, and a tailored blazer, she gives me a genuine handshake and doesn't so much as glance at my bumpy lip.

Her first words when we sit down are: "I hold no expectations from you, Kimberly, other than for you to show up. This is about *your* expectations. What do you hope to get from our time together?"

What are my expectations? No one's ever asked that before. I want to say that I need results, yesterday. That I'm broken and I've tried everything to fix myself and nothing works and I'm out of tricks and just so tired of fighting this same old fight. I want to say that I need for her to be smarter than me, and, more importantly, smarter than my old friend Pain, who is very smart and, apparently, very addictive. But I don't want to sound crazy, right off the bat. I don't want to be committed. My old fantasy of being taken to a hospital and cared for around the clock has dulled since the surgeon slipped me Cs, and I don't want to miss any work.

"We can come back to that one," Andrea says. "Tell me a bit about yourself."

This is the part where I would normally launch into the CliffsNotes version of my horrible childhood. But I decide to start on a positive note, telling Andrea how much I love my stunt work and the financial freedom it gives me. I hope she doesn't think I'm bragging. I just want to send the message, *I'm too successful to be crazy*, even if I'm not sure that's how it works.

But I can't put it off forever, the reason why I'm here, not out there living a happy, free life. So I begin to disconnect. Crossing my ankles, I scrape the toe of my work boot up and down my chair leg. With my senses absorbed in the friction, my self is free to sneak away, like it did at his funeral—and probably lots of times before that. Definitely lots of times since. Floating above, I look down at myself in the chair, hear the squeak of my boot rubbing the chrome leg. I hear my voice telling Andrea the story, but I don't listen to the words.

When it's done, I return to my body. To my surprise, Andrea isn't looking at me like I'm a damaged package on her doorstep. That's a first.

"What you've been through is unthinkable," she says, leaning forward, not away. "But I can already tell you're strong, resourceful, and intelligent. I feel very confident that you will heal."

My glimmer ripples in my chest.

Andrea regards me gently, as if I'm a child. But somehow, I don't feel patronized, I feel seen. "From what you've just told me," she says, "you weren't taught to love yourself, growing up—in fact, quite the opposite. So that's where we'll start."

I squirm in my chair. "Is love really something that can be taught?"

"It is," says Andrea. And then she does a lot of explaining. The gist, if I'm understanding it correctly, is therapy will give me the tools to love myself even when I'm acting in ways that I hate, ways that disgust me. When I'm feeling extreme feelings, acting in extreme ways, Andrea says my inner child has probably been triggered. My "little one," as she also puts it, feels scared and out of control; she's crying out for help. In those moments, I'm supposed to tell the little one stuff like: *It's okay. I'm here, Little Kimberly. You have every right to feel this way. I love you. You're safe.*

I nod. There's no way I'm doing that. It would be a lie. No one is ever safe, obviously. And I don't love my little one. I don't even know her, and I don't especially want to. She's weak and I'm trying to be strong. I don't think I'll ever have the strength to forgive her.

"Maybe for the short term," I say, "you could prescribe an antidepressant?"

Andrea leans back in her chair, blinks a few times, massages her jaw. I can tell she's crafting her response carefully: "I can refer you to a psychiatrist for that, if you like. That said, medication is not usually my first line of defense. My goal is to help you learn how to soothe and care for yourself. Discovering how to do that, from your darkest places, is the essential work we do here."

I nod. "I'm invested. Nothing will change that." My mind flickers to the day of my fall on the *I Am Legend* set—how glorious I'd felt, with my fucked-up, bleeding face. "I just need a little jump start," I finish.

"I hear you," Andrea says. And I think she really does. In spite of her misplaced sympathy for my little one, I like Andrea. After our hour together, I feel the way I do with my old friends, Mary and Michele; the way I did in my SIA group—like I can let my shoulders relax. I feel safe.

It's dark when I leave her office. A light snow falls, and the sidewalks are crowded with people rushing to beat the storm. Everyone is bundled up to their eyeballs, but for once, I'm the not-cold person. I unzip my jacket halfway, let the baby flakes melt on my collarbone. It's like there's a space heater inside me, cranked all the way up. I turn my face to the sky and, on the off chance that this is all her doing, say a quick prayer of thanks to the Virgin Mary. Maybe miracles do happen. Or maybe finding a good a therapist is like buying a bathing suit—you just have to try on a hundred bad ones to find the one that makes you not want to throw up.

15

EPIPHANIES

2008
Thirty-one years old

We are all masterpieces
painted over repeatedly
with enamel conditioning.
It takes patience and courage
to sit still
and chink
the small bits of paint away.
Every so often
a large chunk peels off
like a sunburn.
We get an Aha!
an epiphany
a bigger look at the puzzled mystery.
—Aunt Pat

I keep the poem in my stunt bag, always close, a reminder to keep chipping away at the mystery. Who am I, under the things they painted?

Excuse me, God, if you're there? Why was I given this life, and what am I supposed to do with it?

[Crickets.]

I've come this far. I have a career, adventure, self-sufficiency. So much more than Mom ever got to have. But I didn't go through what I went through to make everyone proud of how well I'm doing with my good job and nice things. I have no desire to feed Grandma Gen's illusion that we all turned out just fine. There has to be a greater plan for me.

I'm in awe of Aunt Pat, for finding her purpose. Last year, she received her doctorate in naturopathy—on top of a master's and a half dozen degrees and certificates in bodywork and natural health. *I'm here to ease suffering, however I can*, she writes to me. And that's what she's always done, as a combat nurse, an aunt, a bodyworker, a healer, a Buddhist. But she's changed in the last few years; after a lifetime of smiling through her pain, like the rest of us, Aunt Pat just smiles now. Her struggle has fallen away.

"I am completely safe when I live in the now and not in my brain or in memories that are long gone," she writes to me. "I am safe when I choose to be free. Life is always a choice, and I choose well-being, creativity, and love."

Aunt Pat believes in nothing more than forgiveness, of herself and others—even him. But I'm not that patient. I'm not that forgiving. I believe forgiveness has to be earned.

What I did inherit is Aunt Pat's curiosity, the need to

understand what happened to us. I've decided the secret to wholeness lies in knowledge. The more information I can collect about our family tree, the stronger my twig will be. So I've been investigating my past. Thanks to the 200 mgs of Zoloft I take every day, I'm a pretty good detective, going about my work with clinical detachment. I can't remember the last time I cried.

What made them like they were? I keep asking. Mom isn't very helpful; her parents never talked to her about their childhoods. Aunt Pat knows the most about Grandma Gen: her father was a cleaner at St. Agnes, and her mother wasn't much of a mother, herself. At eight, Genevieve Mary Shannon was put in charge of her four younger siblings. Every summer morning, her dad dropped them all at Hewlett Point and fetched them at the end of the day. Grandma Gen was beautiful, and told so by her parents. She was her father's "masterpiece," as Aunt Pat once put it—nodding to her own poem, maybe. Genevieve was only sixteen when she met Edward, who put her on a pedestal, exactly where she wanted to be. Married at twenty-one, she went on to have six kids of her own.

Other than being robbed of her childhood, the most telling clue I have about what might have turned Grandma Gen's heart to stone is in a ten-page "biography" she wrote at Aunt Pat's request. After prattling on about her many shining attributes, my grandmother ended her life story with a peculiar little rhyme:

> Why "I am Gen"
> I don't know the answer to give
> Because if I did, it'd be scary to live

But thank you, daughter, dearest Pat
For asking me to write about where I'm at!

I don't know what scared Grandma Gen about her past, what she was afraid to look at. It's tempting to read between the lines, though. Research shows that incest—also called intrafamilial sexual abuse—occurs in more than 10 percent of American families, and is often passed down from generation to generation.

I have little doubt the curse was passed down on *his* side. Everyone remembers that my great-grandmother Tyler, his mother, used to tease her son about how shy he was—so shy, she'd say, laughing, that whenever a certain uncle came to the house, little Ed would hide under the kitchen sink.

Why was he so "shy" around that uncle? No one ever bothered to find out, apparently. What if they had?

...

One sunny Saturday after yoga, I curl into my new white sofa, preparing to call Mom. There are some questions I've been wanting to ask for a long time, and I know they'll sting. Talking about this will tire her out, shut her down, probably ruin her entire day.

It's okay, I remind myself, dialing. Mom is an adult.

She was then, too.

My mother loved me, but she didn't protect me. I need to fill the gap between those two facts. I need to understand what took the mother out of Mom. What cut her off from her memories and instincts so completely that she didn't feel them kicking each time she handed me over?

I know she has answers, locked up behind her steel door, but it's never easy getting to them. I've learned to wear soft gloves as I pick her locks—there are so many locks. Today I start with some chitchat, asking about her day-care business, the weather in Marin, the rom-com she saw with Aunt Pat last week. Then I ask, as delicately as I can: "How long did it go on, for you?"

Mom is quiet for a long time, and I know she's disconnecting from herself, preparing. I wait, looking out on the bright, littered streets of Williamsburg, the Hasidic families walking home from synagogue—little girls in long skirts, walking alongside mothers in shiny brown wigs. Who protects them, I wonder? Are they safer in their world than I was in mine?

"I honestly don't remember, Kim," Mom eventually says, from somewhere faraway.

I move on.

"How far did he go?"

[Silence.]

"My memories are still mostly body memories, Kim."

"Was there"—*Just say it*—"penile rape?"

"No, not that I remember," she says. "That's what he said in his letter, too."

I scrunch up my face. *Stay calm, stay calm, stay calm.* "*What* letter?"

"The one Grandma Gen found, in the crawl space." I hear the sliding glass door to her deck glide open on its tracks, crows squawking, the flare of a lighter, the puff of a Salem Ultra

Light. She only smokes two a day now—though probably more on the days I call.

"Did I not tell you that?" Mom adds.

"You did not." This is not the conversation I planned on having, but a good detective follows her leads where they take her. "You mean the crawl space in the attic?"

[Silence.]

"Mom!"

Little by little, I pull it out of her: After he died, Grandma Gen found a confession letter, shoved deep into the nook behind his drafting table, where he used to work on his architectural drawings and model airplanes. He admitted to molesting children but claimed that he always stopped short of intercourse *because he was so fertile and didn't want to get anyone pregnant.*

"I'm sorry I didn't tell you that before," says Mom. "Maybe it will give you some relief?"

This makes me want to scream, which I can't do, because Mom's steel door is super sensitive, wired to slam shut at loud noises or sudden movements. But excuse me: What kind of monster would brag about his virility while confessing to assaulting children? Also, Mom seems to have forgotten that he forced intercourse on me, the day of my first communion. Given that I was nine, he must have figured pregnancy wasn't an issue.

Now that I've cracked Mom's steel door, all kinds of things are spilling out—stomach-turning details about what else Grandma Gen found in the crawl space. There were Polaroids of boys, naked from the waist down, heads cropped from the frame. There were hand-carved wooden penises. And probably more that wasn't shared. Everything was burned, unsurprisingly, by Grandma Gen.

...

The Zoloft seems to have muted my little one. Maybe it's killed her for good. I can't think why else I'd be so calm right now.

I'm parked outside Earle Avenue again. A year ago, the possibility of going inside—especially around Christmas—would have undone me. A year ago, I would have kept it to the usual holiday drive-by, pulling over to stare for a minute, hand on the latch in case I needed to retch. But here I am, striding up to the house, unfazed.

Was the front path always this short? It used to seem endless, the longest gangplank in the world. Everything is slightly smaller than it should be, out of scale with my memories. It feels as if I've walked onto the studio set of my childhood—but at least I don't have to be small Kimberly anymore.

On either side of the front door, manicured topiaries swirl up from white porcelain planters. The new owners must have real green thumbs to make things grow here. I lift the brass knocker and rap three quick times.

A woman about Mom's age answers the door, wiping a hand on her apron. I make sure to smile as I explain who I am.

"You're Genevieve Tyler's granddaughter?" says the owner. "Such a lovely woman! I know how much she missed your grandfather. He went too young. Would you like to come in?"

"Thank you," I say, stepping inside. "My grandmother will

be so happy to know I saw the house." I'm full of shit. I haven't spoken to Grandma Gen since our meeting in Marin, years ago, and I'm not planning on speaking to her again.

In addition to shrinking the place, the new owners have given it a modern update. The wrought iron chandelier has been replaced by a simple glass one, the beige popcorn-stucco walls Sheetrocked, smooth and light. Through the living room archway, where the tinsel-smothered Christmas tree used to go, a potted ficus twinkles with white fairy lights.

"I've got food on the stove," says the woman. "Feel free to look around!"

I beeline for the basement, gagging only a little as I pass the blue bathroom. I don't need to go in there. I came for the basement, to check out the sight line from the door off the first-floor hallway to his old dungeon below. By seeing it from a grown-up's vantage, I'm hoping I'll finally understand why no one ever saw or heard, how he got away with what he did down there. Especially at parties, right under everyone's dancing feet.

There used to be a thousand stairs, going down forever. I count just eight from the threshold, where I'm standing— where Mom must have stood, the time she could have saved me. There's no view from here. My knees go soft with relief. She couldn't have seen.

It was Christmas, again. I don't know the year, but I know he had me on the bar. I know my white wool tights were pushed all the way down, binding my ankles. I know it was dark, and it felt like I was drowning. And I know that in the middle of it all, Mom cracked the basement door.

Her voice seemed to come from heaven, at first:

"You two okay down there?"

No, Mommy, I'm not okay! I wanted to shout. Why the hell didn't I?

"We're fine, Kath! Just playing a game!" he called up, so cheerfully.

"Okay, come up for cake when you're done!" And she left.

He must have got off me then. It was too close a call, even for him. So we went upstairs, back to the party.

Keep going. You got this. Four more sideways-steps down, and it comes into view: the smooth, polished bar he was so proud of building with his own hands, now stacked with boxes instead of bottles.

Just four more steps. That's all she had to take. But she didn't.

Continuing, I clock the worktable—the very same one, with the side-mounted vise, the shelf underneath for the wood-scrap box—and turn the corner to where the player piano stood. The redbrick wall I remember behind it is now painted glossy white. My eye catches on a pair of letters, down low, carved into one of the bricks.

I crouch on my heels, running my fingers over the painted grooves: ED.

It trips a wire in me, seeing his name, his mark.

There's something I need to do, something I've been fanta-

sizing about for way too long. I run up the stairs and out the
front door, calling a quick "Thank you!" as it slams behind me.

...

The Cemetery of the Holy Rood in Westbury is a twenty-
minute drive from Rockville Centre, but I make it there in
twelve, just before closing time. In the front office, I find his
name in the roster, grab a paper map, and mark an X where he's
buried: Area 13, Range BB, Plot #101. Racing back to my car
before I lose my nerve, I drive along the narrow lanes till I find
the site under a row of blowing oak trees. Grabbing a fat Sharpie
pen from my stunt bag in the trunk, I march up to his grave:

Edward Royall Tyler, 1919–1987
Beloved Husband and Father

Someone has left him flowers, and I stomp on them with
my boot heel before throwing them into the darkness. Trembling, I uncap my pen, kneel, and write in giant capital letters
across the front of the headstone: CHILD MOLESTER. So no
one can miss it, I write it again on the back, then across the
top. *There. Let the world see.*

He hurt children. Everyone knows it, and still, they leave
him flowers, build him shrines, protect him. I've become
certain of it: his acts continue to poison us all. The suffering
won't end, in my family or anyone's, unless we speak up.

So that's what I'll do.

16

NIGHT
AND
DAY

2009
Thirty-two years old

The stunt crew for the action movie *Knight and Day* is top-notch—all the best guys from LA, who've been working together forever. The more they see me work, the more respect they begrudgingly hand over. But it would only take one little mistake to lose them. One mistimed leap or bad landing, and I'd prove they were right. Though no one's said it to my face, I know the story about me: I'm only here because I'm Cameron's friend.

...

Two years ago, I was contemplating a move to LA, where you have to be if you want to "make it" in stunts. Then George Aguilar called: "Don't go just yet, I've got a movie coming up in New York, with Cameron Diaz."

A month later, we were filming the screwball rom-com *What Happens in Vegas*.

I liked Cameron from the moment she stuck out her hand and said, "Hi! I'm Cameron!" She looked directly into my eyes, and I found myself looking right back into hers. Somehow, she made it easy.

I couldn't stop watching her, that first day on set. It was impossible not to. She wasn't just beautiful, she was kind and gracious. Every couple hours she'd look around and say with a laugh, "Guys, don't we have the best job ever?!" No matter who you were—craft service, a grip, a PA—she knew your name. She gave a shit. I didn't meet many people like that.

Late in the afternoon, Cameron had one last costume change to make, and the trailers were far away from the set. "No worries!" she told the crew. "I can do a quick change while the girls cover me, so everyone doesn't have to wait."

Normally, I keep to myself on set, but I mustered the courage to run and grab a stunt mat, then helped her all-female team hold it up as a makeshift dressing room. As we shielded her, giggling like high school girls, I looked around at the others and loved them all instantly.

At the end of the day, I took a chance and handed Cameron my homemade business card, which had a picture of me doing aerial work for AntiGravity.

Cameron gasped. "You do this?"

I nodded. "Before I did stunts, I was a professional acrobat."

"Oh my God, will you teach me?" She was practically jumping up and down.

"I'd be happy to!" Was this really happening?

Cameron grabbed a piece of paper and jotted down a number.

A few days later, I stood waiting for one of the most famous actresses in the world outside of an acrobatics school in Bedford-Stuyvesant. A black town car turned up the industrial, windswept block and out she jumped, greeting me with a big hug. No posse, no bodyguards, just her.

The first step you learn with silks is how to climb to the top, which takes a tremendous amount of upper-body strength and is—as I learned in front of a live audience at the *FHM* shoot years ago—super awkward in the beginning. I figured we would spend the entire session on that one skill, but she shimmied twenty-five feet up to the rafters on her first try.

"Like this?" she called down, beaming.

Oh crap, I thought, looking up at her. *What next?* I ended up teaching her a basic foot lock and a few other moves, which she aced. And we were done.

"Do you have a car coming?" I asked.

Cameron shook her head. "Where's the subway?"

"Oh, you want to take the subway?" Did movie stars know

how to do that? Cameron assured me she always took the train, and we walked together to the station.

"Go," she said, when the eastbound L pulled up first. I shook my head, insisted on waiting to put her on the Manhattan-bound.

Over the course of working together on *Vegas*, and a year later on a psychological thriller called *The Box*, Cameron and I grew closer, bonding over our strong work ethics and bleeding hearts. I learned that she'd left her Long Beach neighborhood behind at sixteen to model, then act. Everything she had, she'd worked her ass off for, too.

But in those first years of our friendship, part of me was afraid Cameron would figure out what a mess I was, emotionally speaking. I'd gone off Zoloft by the time we met and was definitely feeling my feelings again. Plus, I'd started writing down all the gory details of my childhood, filling spiral notebooks and typing them up as chapters in what I hoped would one day amount to a book.

When Cameron asked to see some of my writing, I couldn't help myself. The very next day, I dropped a thick stack of pages—filled with graphic descriptions of my abuse and fantasies of revenge—with her doorman.

The regret swooped in as soon as I left the building. Surely, I'd just doomed our friendship. I was sharing too much, too soon. Now she'd just pity me. Or think I was a psychopath. I couldn't decide which was worse.

But it turned out Cameron thought neither. The next time

I saw her, she told me how sorry she was for what I'd been through. She said she hoped writing it down was cathartic for me, and whenever I wanted to talk, she was there.

Then she said, "So listen! I have this script for a movie with Tom Cruise. Do you want to do it with me?"

...

Two weeks into shooting, in Boston, I'm Cameron's only double for the film, but there are whisperings about them bringing in a more experienced girl for the motorcycle scenes. I get why. I have no experience on bikes, and they want to keep it safe. That said, I'm determined to show them I can handle it, and I've started rehearsing with Jimmy Roberts, Tom's motorcycle double, to get a leg up. I've gotten to know Jimmy pretty well, but Tom's main double, Casey O'Neill, is more of a mystery. What I know about him is what everybody knows: Casey's been doubling Tom for years; he's also considered one of the best stuntmen in the business. Jimmy jokes that he's a ladies' man, but I haven't been paying attention.

I'm still married, after all.

Sorry. There's something I've been leaving out. Someone, that is.

Six years ago, at AntiGravity, I started dating a company member named Shane, a survivor, like me. It was nice never having to explain what it's like to be so broken. We used to joke that we bonded over being damaged goods. Shane and I have stayed together all these years. Not because we make each other happy—we fight like teenagers, always slamming doors and screaming—but because when you've been abused, it's *easy* to stay in unhealthy relationships.

You stay because all the wrong things feel normal and comfortable to you. You tell yourself you're just lucky someone loves you. You see truly happy couples and think, *In another life, I could've had that.*

In this life, eight months ago, I married Shane in a meadow on Mount Tamalpais. A wildfire was burning in the valley below, and I tried not to think of that as a bad omen. It was, though. It's been a dark eight months.

After our last fight, it was clear to me: to continue on with Shane would mean raising children in a household a lot like the one I grew up in—an unhappy one. The night before I came to Boston, I asked for a separation.

Ever since, my phone has been blowing up with Shane's texts and voice mails—pleading at first, then angry. But I've stopped reading or listening to them. My mind is made up: Shane is a good man, but not good for me.

Cameron is always reminding me, "You deserve to be happy." I think I'm starting to believe it.

...

On the final day of the Boston segment, the whole team is supposed to meet for a farewell sushi dinner, but only Casey and I show up. Both of us are tired and looking forward to an early night. I have a 6:00 AM flight to Spain in the morning to shoot the motorcycle scenes I convinced them to let me do. Casey's headed to Austria to film a rooftop fight with Tom.

"How do you meet all these women?" I say to Casey, who's been silencing his buzzing phone all night. "Do you just go around telling people you're Tom Cruise's stunt double, and everyone wants to date you?"

Casey laughs, shaking his head. Okay, he's cute. Older than me, but younger than Tom. Real all-American-looking, and very professional and respectful. A grown-up. In that way, he reminds me of Timmy—but even more of George, who I've come to trust, literally, with my life.

Casey's phone buzzes. I wave my hand. "If you need to go, you can go."

"I'm exactly where I want to be," he replies, putting his phone in his back pocket. "And I was this morning, too."

There's a glint to Casey now. Is he flirting?

This morning was no walk in the park. We filmed a car chase—windows wide open—in ten-degree weather. I was in the back seat in a yellow bridesmaid dress, reaching over a dead guy in the front to (supposedly) drive the car. Casey rode on the roof. We all had blue lips by the end of it.

I slap my credit card down on the table, surprised to hear myself say, "Should we get a drink?"

At a dive across the street, I prop my elbows on the sticky bar and try to look straight at Casey. I've been practicing in the mirror, learning to hold my own gaze, but this is different. Casey is different.

You're not divorced yet, I remind myself, sitting back on my stool. And that's when I see it—across the bar, next to the rows of liquor bottles: a plastic cup of cocktail stirrers.

Just like that, everything good slips away.

I'm back in the basement.

Kimberly, what's your favorite color? He rattles the cocktail stirrers, laughing.

I shake my head so hard I see stars.

Well, then—he grabs the whole fistful—*I'll just have to use them all.*

Pain shoots up my pelvis, up from his world.

"Hey—you okay?" Casey's voice barely registers, but it does. Miraculously, it does.

Head low, I grip the bar. *He's dead, you're safe, he's dead, you're safe*, I tell myself.

"Kimberly?"

I run outside, into the bitter air.

We share a cab in silence—this handsome, normal, undamaged person and me. Casey probably doesn't know what a flashback looks like, but he doesn't ask me to explain. Even stranger, he doesn't try to kiss me. This makes me uncomfortable. Could he possibly not want *anything* for his time and patience tonight? How could that be? It must be an act, to break down my defenses. No wonder he gets all the women.

"Can I walk you in?" he asks, outside my hotel.

I shake my head. Not because Casey's kindness might be a ploy, but because I wouldn't know what to do with him if it wasn't.

17

ONCE UPON A TIME IN SPAIN . . .

2009

Thirty-two years old

Slow and steady, Jimmy circles the bike, herding the nervous animals into the center of the corral. All muscle, bone, and horns, these are not just any bulls, but *toros bravos*, bullfighting stock. Tomorrow, they'll chase us through the streets of Cádiz for *Knight and Day*'s running-of-the-bulls scene. I tap Jimmy's back and point to where a young, mean-looking one stands alone, fixing us with a stare. Jimmy nods but lets the bike idle, not wanting to provoke a chase. They're more dangerous apart than together. At least I think that's what the handlers said. Our "safety course" was presented in a mix of pantomime and Spanish, and I only got the pantomimed parts.

Now, the young one is trotting, head low and snorting, straight for us. "Hold on, Kim!" Jimmy warns, slamming the bike into gear. The front wheel lifts and the bike takes off just as the bull rears up, hooves flying past our unhelmeted heads. We land hard, wobble the tiniest bit, correct, and swerve around the animal as one of the handlers jumps in to wave him off. Another handler swings open the gate, and we race through.

Raphael, the tireless Spanish stunt coordinator, chases after us with a grin. "*¡Oye, bien hecho!* You survived the fiercest one—the top bull!"

Later, thinking of *The Story of Ferdinand* on Collette's childhood bookshelf, I'll ask Raphael what happens if a bull grows up to be more of a mellow, flower-sniffing type. He'll make a quick slashing motion across his throat, gesture cutting and eating with a knife and fork. Poor bulls. They're damned if they fight, damned if they don't. Like every survivor of childhood abuse, I know what that feels like.

...

Past midnight, at the hotel, I sip minibar tempranillo and pace around my tiny balcony, reminding myself of Dad. I usually don't drink the night before a job, but it's better than what I want to do right now. My bulimia has returned, bigtime. The better my career goes, the worse it seems to get. It's never possible to feel skinny enough, in the movie business.

Gripping the balcony with my free hand, I swing one leg over, then the other, so I'm seated on the narrow railing, feet dangling. Three stories down, on the beach, some kids build a bonfire. They see my balancing act, the wineglass in my hand, and look worried. I wave. They wave back. A boy and a girl kick off their jeans and run in their underwear toward the water, which makes me feel slightly queasy. I haven't been in the ocean since middle school, when my fear of the open water got temporarily canceled out by the fun of swimming with Mary and Michele. They both belonged to the Malibu Shore Club in Hempstead, and we spent several summers there, sneaking boxed wine from Michele's mom's cabana, running drunk and laughing into the waves. Then I had my memories and never went into the open water again.

I should sleep—I have hair and makeup in five hours. Instead, I call Mom, whose workday must be just finishing.

"Well, hi!" she answers. "How's—where are you now?"

"Cádiz—southern Spain," I say. "It's pretty, I guess. We're right on the beach in this giant, empty hotel."

"I thought I could hear the ocean," she says. "Sounds nice."

"Mom, did he ever take me sailing or swimming?"

"Who?" she says.

"You know, *him.*"

"Oh." She's silent for a bit. I listen for the flare of her lighter, but the waves are too loud.

"No, I don't think so. Why?"

"I was just wondering why I hate the ocean so much."

"Oh," she says. "Yes, you always did."

I finish my wine. "How's Aunt Pat?"

"She's fine," says Mom. "But . . . forgetful. She completely missed our date to see *Zombieland* last week—and she was *so* excited to see you do your stunts. We're trying again tonight."

"*Awww*," I say. "I know zombies aren't your cup of tea."

"Anything you do is my cup of tea," says Mom.

I must be more exhausted than I think, because Mom's comment about Aunt Pat leaves my mind as soon as we hang up. We're starting to lose her, and neither of us has a clue.

...

In my trailer, Wardrobe, Hair, and Makeup turn me into Cameron's character, June Havens. The white oxford and blue jeans I've worn for the past five days of rehearsals have been laundered and pressed. The brown boots oiled. My hair is June's hair—a ponytail with long wisps pulled loose around the temples. The scars on my forehead are hidden under layers of foundation. My eyes are shadowed in earth tones for June's natural look. I haven't yet felt June's feisty, girl-next-door character seeping into me the way I do when I perform a victim fighting back, though.

Not that it matters. My only job today is to be an acrobat on the back of a bike. It's Cameron's job to be June on the bike. She and Tom will arrive tomorrow to film the same sequences Jimmy and I are about to shoot—minus the most dangerous stunts. Film editors will merge the two versions.

"*¡Buen dia, Brava!*" says Raphael, the coordinator, at my trailer door. "Time to free the bulls!"

Soon, I'm clutching Jimmy's waist as he weaves the bike down a narrow cobblestone street, extras dressed as San Fermín bull runners in red and white scattering around us. The bulls are on our tail, their hoofbeats louder by the second. In an open square, cars drift and swerve across our path, stuntmen popping out of their sunroofs, shooting blanks. The bulls are closing in—I kick one away and we zoom free.

"Two . . . one!" yells Jimmy. I flip around to face him, now riding backward with my spine against the handlebars. More gunshots. I flip back. Flashes of cobblestone, a camera car, rooftops, sky. Through my clenched teeth, I'm beaming.

"Thank you for keeping me alive," I tell Jimmy, hours later, raising my shot glass.

"Same." He salutes me back.

Too exhausted to talk, I study the pictures on the bar wall behind him—men with bodies like dancers, some being gored, some doing the goring. Someone touches my shoulder. I twirl around, chair scraping, fists clenched.

"Casey!" I practically jump into his arms, inhaling his grassy cologne. "What are you doing here?"

"I came to see you," he says.

The little black box of fear I've been carrying around, wedged tightly between my upper ribs, instantly vaporizes. Since Boston, Casey and I have been texting nonstop, but I haven't heard from him in two days. I know he's been busy wrapping the Austria shoot, but I was starting to believe the mean little voice inside me that said: *Guys like him don't stay with girls like you.*

But now he's here, standing in front of me, real.

I pack my things, and we drive along the peninsula to a faded-elegant hotel in the next town, with stained glass skylights and dusty chandeliers. At the center of the lobby is a grand, red-carpeted staircase, but I go straight to the brass-doored lift. I'm not ready for Casey to see what a freak I am about stairs yet.

Our room is small but lavish. I push aside gold velvet drapes and open the bay windows facing the water and a shuttered boardwalk. All of southern Andalusia's beach towns are empty this time of year, and I get the feeling we might have the entire place to ourselves. I move around, dimming lights, pulling down the brocade cover on our Gothic four-poster bed.

Casey emerges from showering in a plush robe, falling onto the white sheets. He must be exhausted, after nearly twenty-four hours of travel from Austria to Sevilla to Cádiz to wherever we are. My day has felt infinite, too, but I'm lit up with nervous energy. We've never been this alone before, never even properly kissed. Impulsively, I climb on top of him, holding his wrists and meeting his lips.

I let Casey flip me over. Now he's on top, looking down at me. We're both panting a little, wondering what's next. I know what I want. I want him, completely. No part of me—body, brain, or soul—doesn't want Casey right now. This makes me feel frighteningly vulnerable. I feel myself disconnecting, my body starting to shake. Waves of heat roll through me, and I can't find my breath.

"I think—I think I'm going to pass out."

Casey jumps off me. "I'll get some water."

He sits on the edge of the bed, giving me space, while I drink the glass down. We stay like that for a while, listening to the surf through the open windows.

"I'm fine," I say.

"I know," says Casey. "Should we go to sleep?"

I nod, focusing on the moon over the water. "It wasn't you. I'm sorry."

"You don't need to say that," says Casey. "I've noticed you say that a lot."

About to apologize for apologizing too much, I hold Casey's palm to my cheek instead.

By the time I've taken a bath (to avoid closing the shower curtain), Casey is fast asleep, the velvet drapes pulled closed, muffling the ocean. He's taken the side that's close to the wall, leaving me the window side with the pretty nightstand and the little bouquet of roses and glowing library light. He's given me the good side, because one of the millions of facts he doesn't know about me is that other people's good things aren't always so good for me. I can't sleep near windows, open or not. It doesn't matter that he came in through the door; windows are easier to break.

I consider waking Casey and asking him to move over. But what if he asks why? He'll think I'm crazy. So I curl up on the "good" side, on high alert. I should be able to do this. I'm thirty-two years old for chrissakes.

Time slides, blue dawn creeps around the curtains. . . .

I jolt awake in daylight, heart punching, legs scrambling in the sheets. There's a man in my bed.

"It's me, it's me, it's me," he says.

Casey. I collapse with relief.

"Do you want to tell me what's going on?" he asks, after another glass of water.

I'm quiet awhile. Obviously, my best hope of keeping him around is not to tell him what's going on—*It was so much worse than you think; I'm very fucked up*—but to bring back the Kimberly he met in Boston. Feisty-Survivor Kimberly. It's *La Brava* he fell for, not me. But what does Aunt Pat say? "*Courage is being scared and doing it anyway.*"

"Let's go to the beach," I say.

It's blustery outside. I hold my fluttering journal closed, showing Casey the cover. I invested in a good one this time—soft tan leather with a gold border. On the front cover, I've written BTC, for "breaking the cycle," like the tattoo I got on my wrist last year. Under that, I've taped a photo of myself, age seven or eight, standing onstage at a dance recital with two other little girls. I'm wearing a blue tutu, a tiara, and a small, wary smile. The others, in their identical costumes, hold their hands loosely by their sides, but mine are clenched in fists, like I'm ready for a fight.

In the three weeks I've been in Spain, I've already filled half the leather book with my bubbly handwriting, which hasn't changed much since I was that girl. I'm not sure I've changed much, either. Not quite hyperventilating, I place my life in Casey's hands.

The truth will set you free.

I do cartwheels up and down the shore to keep myself from exploding while he reads, slumped over the blowing pages. When he's done, Casey jumps up and hugs me, the tide hushing in our ears. "I'm so sorry," he says.

"Thanks," I say, and we walk in silence—good, close, loving silence—back to the hotel.

"Race you to our room?" he says, in the lobby. I run for the elevator as he heads for the stairs. I jab the brass button, but nothing happens. There's no time!

The stairs are my only chance to win, so I take them—eyes forward all the way up.

18

A WARRIOR'S WISDOM

2010
Thirty-three years old

I never knew Los Angeles had wide-open places left, but we've driven for miles without passing a single car; nothing but oaks and swooping hawks and occasional tall gates protecting hidden oases—the last one a couple miles back now. Casey swerves his truck around a dead rabbit, turns up a dirt road, and pulls to a stop.

"This is it!" he says. Killing the engine, he turns to me, beaming. "What do you think?"

I shield my eyes against the hard white sun and take in Casey's property—a construction site on a flattened hilltop looking out on a wide-open canyon. Is it beautiful or barren? Promising or unwelcoming? I can't decide.

"Are there hyenas here?" I end up saying.

"Hyenas?" Casey laughs, shaking his head. "It's not the Serengeti, Kim."

I relax a little, until he adds, "Coyotes and mountain lions, though."

Reluctantly, checking for snakes, coyotes, and mountain lions, I follow Casey across the dry field and into a half-built, Mediterranean-style home, so big it could hold the house on Skillman four times over. "The garage and gym will go down the hill," says Casey, pointing through an empty window frame.

"And the pool?" I ask.

Casey shrugs. "Not planning on one."

"Oh, you've gotta have a pool," I say, touching my sweaty neck. "I'd put it right there."

Casey grabs me around the waist. "Don't go back to New York. Live with me. We'll build this home together."

I pull away, heart kicking, and briefly consider bolting off down that dusty road. But it's miles to the bottom, and that would definitely look crazy. Normal people don't run like hell from kindness, from love. Even I know that. I pick up a baseball-size rock and, winding up like Dad taught me when I was still in diapers, pitch it into the distance.

"I told you. I need to stand on my own feet."

"You will," says Casey. "Next to me. And your feet can walk away anytime you tell them to, you know."

I look for another rock to hurl. He's said the "right" thing again, which makes me suspicious. Maybe Casey really is too good to be true.

I've seriously entertained the idea that he's a killer disguised as the perfect boyfriend; it would make more sense than this relentless . . . niceness. He told me once that when we first met and he heard I was married, he thought, *The good ones are always taken.* He said he couldn't believe his luck when he found out I was separated. Casey is the third person I've ever fallen in love with. Sometimes I think I'm still recovering from the first.

That would be Nick, who came to Oceanside High shortly after I had my memories. I loved every detail about him—not just the important fact that Dad hated him. I loved Nick's curly brown hair, long and unwashed; his jeans that rested too low on his hips; his after-school bookie job; and his dented white Camaro with a T-top, always blasting The Pharcyde.

Nick would've been the boy I lost my virginity to, if that hadn't already happened. *No kissing,* he informed me, the first time. Then, after: *What happened back there, I could have done to a balloon. It doesn't mean anything.* Then, for the entire year we were "together": *No one can know about this.* So our relationship was carried out in private, away from the prying eyes of our classmates.

Nick made sense to me, affirmed my view of myself, and the world. As a girl, as myself, I was the object, not the subject, of desire. Sexual encounters were supposed to be secrets. Nick was the love I deserved.

Good therapy has taught me that I deserve better. Everyone deserves to mean *something.* But if Casey is looking for a healthy, stable partner and not someone to kill in her sleep, reading my journal should have set him straight: It was no stroke of luck, finding me. He picked the wrong suitcase. Wouldn't it be selfish to stay here with him, to waste his time? Like I said to Andrea in our last phone session, sooner or later, he'll discover me huddled in the shower and realize what he's in for, and it will all be over anyway, so what's the point?

Andrea said love doesn't work that way. I don't believe her, but I'm not selfless enough to leave the best guy I've ever been with, so I tell Casey, "Fine, I'll stay. I'll help you build it. But only if I can get regular work here."

It's a built-in escape hatch. The stunt world is so much bigger in LA, so cutthroat and competitive. I tell myself I'll be flying home to New York within the month.

...

I can't fail. I can't leave. It feels right to be here. Not the falling-in-love part, which is as uncomfortable as it is exciting, like wearing a fabulous Oscars gown cut for someone else's body. And not because I particularly like LA. I don't sync with the slow-motion California energy, and my whiny Long Island accent announces "outsider" every time I open my mouth. The reason I'll never use my escape hatch back to New York is that LA is clearly my next career step, and I'd rather die than stand still. Besides, not fitting in is my natural state.

Within days of packing up my Williamsburg apartment and filing for divorce, I book my first Hollywood job, doubling the actor Yvonne Strahovski on an episode of the TV show *Chuck*. My excitement turns into anxiety, though, when I find out that I'll be fighting Zoë Bell, only the greatest stuntwoman alive. I'm going to get annihilated.

We're supposed to be rival models at a fashion show, out for each other's blood, but Zoë—costumed like me in a tiny dress and towering stilettos—greets me on set like an old friend.

"Hi there, love!" she says in a pretty Kiwi accent. "Ready to rehearse?"

All my eye-contact progress goes right out of the window. "It's an honor to meet you," I tell Zoë's shoes, close to bowing. "You were so, so amazing in *Kill Bill*."

"Aw, thanks, yeah," she says, waving away the compliment. "Busted my ribs on that one, but well worth it! If it weren't for that movie, I'd have been back in New Zealand three months after I left! Haven't you doubled for Uma, too?"

I nod, feeling 10 percent less nervous. Zoë was once an outsider, too. "*My Super Ex-Girlfriend* was my first job ever," I say.

"Not bad, then!" says Zoë. "Let's see what you've got—and don't be afraid to hurt me, yeah?"

No risk of that. I know next to nothing about fighting. But if Zoë is appalled, she doesn't show it. After an afternoon of throwing me around the catwalk, she walks me to my trailer and teaches me how to do a proper side kick against the wall. "Practice that over and over, and you'll be right set!"

I nod, trying to match her optimism. "Thank you. You've been so nice. I just have"—my voice catches—"so much to learn."

"Hey," says Zoë. "I'm still learning, too." She runs a hand through her daisy-blond hair, thinking for a minute. "Just know yourself, Kim. Know what you're worth, and where you're going. I've no worries about you!"

That makes one of us.

As I drive home, committing Zoë's wisdom to memory—*know yourself, know your worth, know where you're going*—a surreal thought pops into my head: What if Hollywood isn't so cutthroat, after all? What if it's full of kind, good-hearted people who can help me bloom?

I don't realize it yet, but by simply considering that possibility, I'm allowing it to happen. Zoë, for one, will become a fast friend, and a frequent on-screen collaborator. Eight years in the future, as the stunt coordinator for Quentin Tarantino's *Once Upon a Time in Hollywood*, she'll hire me to be part of the final, ensemble fight sequence with Brad Pitt (and a scene-stealing pit bull). In that one, I'm the redheaded Manson Girl who tackles Brad on a table before he smashes my head into various things—a telephone, a framed Western movie poster, a wall, etc.—until I'm good and dead. Though seemingly brutal and chaotic, that scene will be as tightly choreographed as a ballet. We'll spend months preparing for it—the breakaway phone tested, the lunges, punches, slashes, and smashes rehearsed until we could do them in our sleep. And some nights, dreaming, I do.

Zoë's artfulness, her team's attention to detail and safety, will make me start to rethink my relationship with my craft, and also with my old friend Pain. At last, I'll approach stunt work as a professional, not someone looking to get hurt.

...

Know where you're going. That's the easiest one. I'm going up in the stunt world. Which means I need to learn how to fight properly. Thinking of all those years I wasted on cheap therapy when the good stuff was beyond my reach, I decide to invest in private tae kwon do lessons with the best of the best.

Grand Master Shin, who goes by Charlie because he has nothing to prove, is a seventh-degree black belt. Born in Korea, he learned from his father, a ninth degree. Charlie is old school—strict and tough as blocks, familiar. At my first lesson, I show him the side kick Zoë taught me against my trailer wall. When he folds his arms and says, flatly, "We have work to do here," I know I've found my guy.

Charlie's gym has a trampoline and a spring floor, which lets us combine flipping, kicking, and punching into my training. Some days it feels as if I'll never get better; others it feels as if I'm getting worse. But over time, we add snap kicks, hook kicks, spinning hook kicks, and tornado kicks to my arsenal, all while brushing up on my gymnastics and training me out of the open postures that years of dance trained into me.

It doesn't take long for me to realize that Charlie is giving me much more than tools for my work. It's healing to fight in the real sense of the word, not in a desperate, flailing attempt to survive, but on my terms, with strategy, calm, and patience.

In martial arts, as in yoga, breath is everything. Breathing into my punches and kicks strengthens them, and me. I realize that I've been holding my breath my whole life, thinking this would protect me, hold my world together, when the opposite was true. *Just breathe.* It's been Aunt Pat's mantra for years, and now it's mine, too. *Just breathe* on the mat. *Just breathe* through the audition. *Just breathe* at the endless red light. *Just breathe* when you wake yourself up, thrashing and screaming, at 2:00 AM.

I've been having a recurring nightmare about my abuser. He's just the same—half drunk, sometimes savagely so, flushed and devil-eyed and coming for me in the dark. Only, I'm not the little one anymore. I'm the adult, and I'm stronger than him. It's *my* turn to be the destroyer. But the first rule of stunt fighting, no contact, stops every punch and kick just short, sparing him. I'm not allowed to hurt my demon in my nightmares—it's my *job* not to hurt him. How messed up is that?

Just breathe, I'll tell myself at my next lesson, picturing his head on the paddle or punching bag as I decimate it.

If my abuser were alive, I'd probably torture him, shove dirt in his mouth, and bury him alive. But he's dead, so I'll never get to kill him, let alone confront him. On the bright side, this frees me up to embrace the deeper practice of tae kwon do, which at its core is about kicking ass with respect—respect for your opponents, and also for yourself. All these years that I've been a gymnast, a dancer, an acrobat, and a stuntwoman, I've been using my body as a tool for escape. But martial arts is teaching me how to use my body as a tool for presence. I stand up straight, now, when I enter a room. I stop talking to people's feet and look them in the eyes, including when it's hard. And I no longer wear headphones all the time. Without music blasting in my ears, I'm forced to be with myself—to just *be*.

Know yourself. Does that mean your whole self? Your young self, too? We'll get there.

Know your worth. This is happening, already. I'm coming to understand that I am more than a body, more than the sum of my pain. I must be, or why would someone like Casey want me around? Why would Cameron and her inner circle have welcomed me in? Every month or so, a group of us meet at Cameron's for what we call a seven-hour salad, which is not just a wholesome bowl of greens. Cameron (in her beloved Meat visor) mans the grill, and we talk and eat the day away, feeding our stomachs and feeding our souls.

Still, I cry almost every day, my first year in LA. Mostly out of exhaustion. Between training with Charlie five days a week, looking for work, ironing out my divorce settlement, and helping Casey manage the contractors, it takes all I have left to act like a regular girlfriend.

I love telling Casey about my day, love falling asleep in his arms. But some nights before bed, I wish I could wrap myself in bubble wrap, make my vagina disappear. There's no leaving my body anymore during sex—or what's the point in being here at all? After so many years of faking intimacy with other partners, staying present can take the will of a grand master.

It's not just me who's learning how to do this relationship. Casey can forget that I'm dealing with my past, on some level, every second of every day. After years in the stunt world, his attitude toward pain in general is *bandage it up and work through it.* He doesn't get that some kinds of pain don't allow for that.

"But you're the strongest person I know," he says, when the house on the canyon is finished and I refuse to sleep on the window side of the bed. It takes a joint session with Andrea for Casey to understand that the best way he can help me to move forward is to respect my choices, not to tell me how he'd handle them.

Even with Andrea's help, Casey is slightly mystified by my need to have a relationship with my parents. How I can forgive them for what happened, their neglect. As a dad himself—Casey has a teenage daughter—it's inconceivable to him that my mom and dad didn't protect me from my abuser. It's particularly difficult for Casey to put himself in Mom's shoes. It was one thing for her to repress her own abuse memories; it was another to keep them locked up behind her steel door when they could have saved me.

Anyone who's been where Mom and I have probably knows that trauma memories—often hidden away in our cells, where we can't see them—don't work like that. You can't muscle them out of hiding if you have no idea they exist in the first place. They come out when they decide it's time. Memory repression is a form of dissociative amnesia, a verified disorder in the *Diagnostic and Statistical Manual of Mental Disorders, Fifth Edition*. It's now recognized as a common response to trauma, particularly in sexual assault survivors. This is despite widespread media bias against the phenomenon—a shaming, silencing bias that was created and fed for nearly two decades by an influential organization called the False Memory Syndrome Foundation (FMSF). Founded in 1992 and finally dissolved in 2019, FMSF was (no surprise here) founded by a man, Peter Freyd, whose adult daughter had recovered memories of her own child sexual abuse—at his hands.

Which brings me back to Dad not recognizing my abuse,

and not believing me when I finally spoke out. Casey can't understand how he didn't see the signs. But knowing what Dad went through in Vietnam—after a rough childhood of his own—I can. Dad thought he was dealing with life just fine, but I witnessed every day of my childhood how the pain he carried home from the war numbed him, closed him off. Because I relate to his trauma, I get why he couldn't see what was happening right under his nose. Which is why I've forgiven him. For that, at least.

When every room in the new house has been painted and all the bells and whistles—except the pool, a work in progress—are in place, I tell Casey I want to invite Dad for a visit.

"Are you sure you're up for that?" he says, like I knew he would.

"I'm sure," I answer.

I haven't spoken to Dad since I called to tell him I was divorcing Shane, over a year ago.

"But you made a vow," he'd said, sounding like a confused seven-year-old. "It's only been a year!"

Dad was so crushed, I felt a little guilty for taking his friend away from him. Shane *was* fun at parties. Then it hit me: yet again, Dad was siding with a drinking buddy over me.

"Bye, Dad, love you!" I hung up.

Casey doesn't give a damn that my family is Team Shane. My boyfriend, like all the people I'm choosing to surround myself with now, is Team Kimberly. He's not too good to be true, it turns out. He's just plain *good*. I am someone he loves, and he wants what's best for me, which we both know is not

spending time with Dad. The visit will cost me, but I don't
care. Whatever the price, no matter how many weeks it'll take
to right myself afterward, I want Dad to see who I've become,
all on my own.

So Dad comes, and Casey is a warm and generous host. I
trail along as he leads Dad on the grand house tour.

My father is briefly speechless. As a mason, nothing gets
his heart beating like a quality-built house, and I haven't seen
him get this emotional since we visited Aunt Pat's sturdy
modern ranch in Lagunitas, back in my half-drawn years.

"Aww, kids," says Dad, choking up. "You done real, real
good."

Every detail—The plaster crown molding! The half-bullnose
edging on the granite countertops! The automatic light in the
walk-in pantry!—is acknowledged, appreciated. Seen.

If only we'd ended the visit there. But no. I had to stock the
fridge with rum, Coke, and Coors Light (for Dad) and pinot
grigio (for me).

After cleaning up our takeout feast, I climb onto my beautiful kitchen island with its half-bullnose-edge granite coun-
tertop and cross my legs.

"Why didn't you believe me in high school, Dad?"

"In high school?" Dad stops examining the tile work on
our backsplash and turns to face me, incredulous. "It was college! And I did believe you!"

"I had my memories when I was fifteen, Dad. You said I
got them from a book."

"Kim, please. There was a lot going on. Your mom and I—"

"Why do you only believe what you can see with your eyes?

Why can't you trust? Why did it take this house for you to be proud of me?"

"I've always been proud of you, Kim."

"But you didn't believe me. Why would a child make that up?"

"Kim, if you'd said it when he was alive, I woulda killed him. You know that, right? I woulda shot him dead right on his front stoop. I don't care if I went to jail forever, I woulda killed that son of a bitch. You know that, right?"

"Yeah, I know," I lie, because I'm tired and want to go to bed. And also because that's how Dad does it, how he survives.

...

A few days after Dad's visit, I drive to the County Planning Department to submit the drawings for our swimming pool. Having failed to sell practical Casey on the idea, I've decided to have one put in myself. I'm making real money in LA, and it doesn't seem like a big deal to pay to get what I want.

But moments after delivering the plans, doubt sets in: What am I doing? What reassurance do I have that I'll be with Casey long enough to swim in this damn pool? Where is this relationship going? What is it worth to me? To Casey? If I did want him to care for me for the rest of my life, as I can now see caring for him, would that be weak? Or would it be the bravest choice I've ever made?

I want a new family, built on transparent love. No more bluffing to survive.

It's the middle of the night in Dubai, where Casey has gone to film *Mission: Impossible—Ghost Protocol*. I call him anyway, from a bench outside the planning department.

"Kim?" he rasps. "You okay?"

I take a deep breath.

19

TO LOVE
YOU MORE
THAN
YESTERDAY

2012–2014

Thirty-five to thirty-seven years old

If this is not a dream, I'm standing on a wide stone terrace on the Amalfi Coast—the turquoise, yacht-flecked sea glittering below. Only, I'm not exactly standing, more like hovering, just millimeters above the ground. For once, I'm lifting with joy, floating in my body, not away from it.

Casey stands opposite me in a crisp white dress shirt that sets off his blue eyes and olive skin, tanned from our drive to Positano—convertible top down, scooters whizzing by, my creamy scarf billowing in the wind. I've traveled the world for work, but this, our wedding-slash-honeymoon, is my first-ever vacation. I keep forgetting: I'm here just to *be*.

But seriously—I take in the rippling cypress trees, the hot pink bougainvillea tumbling from the balcony railing, the faint chime of teacups on the hotel patio, invisible below us—is this a Bond movie set, or my life? Our officiant and only witness, a young Italian woman in a simple yet perfectly tailored suit, is too pretty and put together not to be an actor. She closes the leather-bound book in her hands, gives Casey a solemn nod, and he begins to read from the vows he's written on the thick hotel stationery.

"I will hold your hand today," Casey tells me, "the same as when I'm old and wrinkly. I will always love you more than yesterday. . . ."

Yes, this is my life. Yes, I deserve this happiness, this unconditional love.

It's my turn. I take a long breath of the warm, lemony air, brush away a tear, then another. I give up and let them fall. "Thank you for seeing me as I am," I say to Casey, "and loving every part of me." I tell him that with him by my side, I know it's going to be alright. It already is. The present is so bright, I realize, it's outshined my family's absence.

Taking this step without them hadn't felt right, but neither had taking it with them. I sense that Dad and Collette think I gave up on my first marriage, didn't try hard enough. My endless pursuit of happiness, my refusal to give up on *myself*, might look like selfishness to them. But I know it's not.

Struggle and sacrifice make a good Marine. But that's not what got me here. My glimmer did.

"Hey, let's jump in the water!" says Casey, as we pose for pictures. He turns to the photographer. "Can we do that?"

I look to the photographer, hoping he'll say it's too dangerous. But he says there's a lower cliff that local kids jump from. He tells us that in Italy, a wet wedding is good luck. *Shit*.

I look down at my beautiful dress that shimmers like rose quartz. I look *way* down at the Mediterranean, lapping gently against the rocks, and wobble on my feet. I've done openwater scenes for movies, but this will be *me* jumping in, not *La Brava*. My mind cuts to Mary, Michele, and me, squealing with laughter in the pounding Long Island surf.

"Okay," I tell Casey, slugging the last of my champagne. "But backward."

The picture that comes in the mail, a month later, will be worth the ruined dress. Hands in the air, we're suspended in tandem, whooping—the shining water and cliffs behind us. I will frame and hang it, along with our vows, in our entryway, a reminder to accept my happiness, because it is mine. My choices—good, bad, ugly, all mine—brought me to that leap.

...

A year later, I'm landing hard.

"There's no way it's alive!" I moan to my gynecologist, holding my head. "Oh God, what did I do?"

I just found out I'm seven weeks pregnant—and I've been

doing stunts that could have killed me, let alone the delicate fetus I didn't know I was carrying.

Let me back up . . .

Having a baby was the last thing on my mind. Casey and I had only talked kids once, vaguely. I'd said—without getting into it—that I was unsure whether I wanted to be a mom; Casey looked relieved, saying he couldn't picture being a new dad at his age. We'd left it at that.

I was filming a vampire movie called *Freaks of Nature*. One day on set, a fellow stuntwoman who I've become close with over the years turned to me and said, out of the blue, "So are you guys going to have kids, or what?"

I remember looking down at my body when she said that. I was wearing a red-and-black-plaid baby doll dress—a duplicate of the one worn by Mackenzie Davis, an otherworldly twentysomething actress I'd starved myself to double. I was lean and muscular, sculpted by hundreds of hours of tae kwon do, biking, running, hiking, Pilates, and hot yoga. This was the body my job demanded; there was no room in it for feeding and sheltering another body. Having a baby would mean taking myself off the market for nine months, plus recovery time, plus getting-back-in-shape time, at the very moment my career was booming. Everyone knows it's out of sight, out of mind, in Hollywood.

"Maybe one day," I told my friend, with a shrug. "But now seems like a bad time."

A veteran stuntwoman with grown kids, she gave me a

motherly look. "Kim, no time is going to feel right, in our business. If you want a family, you should just start trying. At thirty-five, it could take a while. You know that, right?"

Did I know that? Yes and no. Over the years, I'd scrolled past women's magazine headlines about the fertility problems of "older" women who'd put off motherhood for their careers, the rise in IVF treatments, the great "insurance policy" that is egg freezing. But having spent my prime reproductive years lurching from flashback to flashback, there hadn't been much headspace left over to consider my biological clock.

Suddenly, its ticking was deafening, and I knew what I hadn't been letting myself know: I yearned to be a mom. And the yearning was bigger than the terror that I would fail (like I apparently have). The very evening of my conversation on set, Casey and I had unprotected sex, never dreaming that I'd get pregnant on the first try.

"You would have miscarried by now, if you were going to," the doctor tells me, with infuriating calm.

"You don't understand!" I plead, digging in my purse for the evidence. "Can I just show you what I'm talking about?" Pulling my phone from under the ziplock baggie holding the three positive home pregnancy tests I took before calling the doctor, yesterday, I open up a video of me doing a thirty-foot ratchet onto the hood of a car (meaning I was tied to cables powered by an air-pressure cylinder, which propelled me onto that hood with extra force). "I did this numerous times," I say, holding the evidence right up to the doctor's face, where he can't miss it.

He winces as my body splinters the protective windshield. "*Ooof*," he says, watching me lift myself up, bloodied.

"That's what I'm saying to you!" I tell him, twisting my hands. "I've already quit the film. But what now?"

Somehow, the doctor remains positive. "You assume the best," he says, "and take care of yourself."

Like the good student I've never been, I frantically write down his instructions about sonograms and folic acid and not jumping through windshields and the extra tests available to women of my "advanced maternal age." *Yes, Doctor; whatever you say, Doctor. Grant me this second chance, and I will protect my child with my life, for the rest of my life. I will get this right.*

"Oh!" I remember, as God, I mean the doctor, checks my pulse. "Can you please make a note that I want an unmedicated birth? I don't want drugs." *How sweet the pain of bringing new life into the world must be.*

The doctor shuffles through my file, snaps it closed. He informs me with an apologetic look: "Typically, as a precaution with herpes patients, we deliver by caesarean." If there's an active outbreak during a vaginal birth, he explains, the baby could be born blind.

I bite my cheek, hard. "I won't have an outbreak. I'll take good care of myself."

It wasn't until my twenties that I figured out, thanks to Planned Parenthood, I had both kinds of herpes. The "yeast infections" of my school days—too much time in those sweaty tights and leotards—had been something else.

No matter how much self-care I do, and I do it all— prenatal yoga, long gentle walks, spinach-and-kale shakes with double shots of wheat grass (Aunt Pat's recommended elixir), relaxing music at all times, and so on—my hormones trigger wave after wave of herpes flare-ups throughout my pregnancy. Each time a new episode announces itself with a shooting pain down my leg, I'm overcome with fresh rage and self-pity. Lying in bed with an ice pack between my legs, lidocaine numbing everything *but* the pain, I try, in vain, to let go of the birth I'd imagined.

For once in my life, I want to take a step forward without the past jerking me back.

But as the months pass, my fantasy that motherhood will give me a new outlook on life seems increasingly ridiculous. We get a dozen good test results, but when the doctor raises one eyebrow during a sonogram, I spiral. *What isn't he saying? It's the fucking ratchet, I know it!*

And my real fear: What if nothing I do will be enough to protect this child? What if the curse of Earle Avenue follows my baby, too?

Of all the coping skills Andrea's taught me in our years of working together, surrender has been the toughest to grasp. I cannot let go of Worry, any more than Anger. What I do surrender is my fear of gaining weight. For the first time in nine years, there is no ideal woman to double; for the first time in twenty years, I don't want to punish my body for what it knows. I want to love it, feed it, nurture it. Nurture *us*. So I surrender to my cravings, and surrender some more. I gain seventy-two pounds, which makes the doctor worry about gestational diabetes.

"You can stop gaining now," he says.

"Maybe we should calm down on the burritos?" Casey suggests.

The two of them stare at me on the examining table with matching looks of concern, but I'm not concerned. I only eat when I'm hungry. I'm following my body's lead on this one.

"No," I say, cinching my paper robe with a steely smile. "I don't want to. And I will not have this conversation with two men."

...

Three weeks before my scheduled caesarean, Casey leaves me to my craving and worrying to take his first stunt-coordinating job in New Orleans. But it's all planned out: He'll be home in time for the birth of our baby girl—I don't need a test to tell me that's what she is, I just know.

My water breaks two weeks early, in the middle of the night.

I've got a Birth Plan B, of course. And a Birth Plan C. Plan B is for my friend Lee-Anne to take Casey's place. Lee-Anne and I met filming *Jack Reacher*. She's also a stuntwoman, one of the best, so I figured the two of us together could execute the Plan like ninjas. Not exactly. We're more like Abbott and Costello, bumbling around my living room, shoving unnecessary items into my already-packed go bag. Somehow, we arrive at the hospital without our wallets (Lee-Anne remembers only her lip gloss and phone). But we make it, with time to spare.

"My girlfriend is parking the car," I tell the check-in nurse. From that moment on, everyone at the hospital thinks that Lee-Anne is my romantic partner, and I let them, because I want to make sure they'll let her in the birthing room. Like the seven-hour salad girls, Lee-Anne is part of my new family—the one I get to choose, and the one I'm counting on to show me how to do this. As much as I want Mom and Dad in my child's life, I know they can't teach me to be the kind of parent I want to be. I've made peace with that.

"I'll show your wife in," says the physician's assistant, once I've gotten my epidural.

"Please hurry!" I call, as she bustles from the room. But the door hasn't even closed when Lee-Anne bursts through it.

"What can I do?" she gasps, rushing to my bed. "What do you need? Music? Socks?" She reaches into her jeans pocket, producing the lip gloss with a sheepish shrug: "Nars Orgasm?"

Laughing, but deadly serious, I grab her so hard my IV twists in my wrist.

"When this baby comes out, whatever you do, do *not* let it out of your sight. Not for a second. Promise?"

"I promise," says Lee-Anne, squeezing my hand. "Not for a second."

And for that moment, at least, I know it: my baby is not cursed. She is protected. She is blessed.

20

BREAKING
THE SCALE

2014
Thirty-seven years old

I'm vibrating with adrenaline as I type the words into the search window: *breastfeeding, flashbacks.*

My body quiets down as soon as the results appear on my screen: pages and pages of links to studies and blogs and mommy forums devoted to the topic of breastfeeding after sexual abuse. So I'm not a freak, not the only woman to convulse with flashbacks every time I put my baby to my breast.

I'd been looking forward to nursing my daughter—named Capri, after the place where Casey and I chose love over all else. It had gone so well, at the hospital, when I was numbed by the painkillers. I'd had my saline C cups replaced by more realistic silicone Bs not long before getting pregnant, and the minute Capri latched on, I was struck by how right, how natural, we looked together. At last, my body seemed to be at peace with itself, at one with its purpose. But the first time we tried nursing at home, my abuse memories surged up from deep inside me, played themselves on the screens of my eyelids till I screwed up my face and disconnected my baby, gently, painfully, from my body.

Apparently, it's a stimulation thing.

The closeness, the sensations, the feeling of giving one's body over to another can trigger flashbacks, stress hormones, even dissociation. It's not just nursing that's harder for new moms like me. We're also more likely to experience anxiety, depression, hypervigilance, and feelings of shame and inadequacy—in short, everything I've felt since the minute I found out I was pregnant.

The most important matter is protecting Capri, this perfect baby that I increasingly feel I do not deserve and do not know what to do with, other than keep alive and happy and uncontaminated by my issues.

For both our sakes, I stop breastfeeding and buy a pump. Every two hours, I hand my tiny girl to Lisa, the doula who's saving me from myself. I strap on the milking machine and distract myself from the shitstorm of sensations and memories by lifting seven-pound hand weights.

"I'm still mad as hell about it," I say to Andrea on the phone. When Capri came, and I felt myself turning into someone I did not quite recognize, I upped my therapy to twice a week.

"How are you doing otherwise?" she asks. "Is your mom there?"

"She just left," I whisper, looking into the nursery as Lisa rocks Capri in her bassinet. When Lisa straightens up, I mouth, *Stay with her.* She gives me a thumbs-up, shoos me out.

"I'm terrified that she'll die in her sleep," I tell Andrea. "I'm terrified to leave her alone with anyone but Casey or Lisa, at least before she has a voice."

"Did you let your mom hold Capri?" asks Andrea. There she goes, circling back to Mom.

"Of course!" I answer, fake brightly, hoping that will satisfy her. I wish we didn't have to talk about Mom. It was nice to have her here, but it was also . . . complicated. Too complicated to explain, even to Andrea.

I can't help being mad at Mom for how hard this is. For not protecting me like I will protect Capri. For not showing me how to do that. My childhood is already haunting my daughter's, and I can't talk to Mom about it for fear of hurting *her* feelings.

"Was your mom fearful about safety when you were young?" asks Andrea.

I snort. "She was the opposite of my dad! I don't think she let me cross the street alone till I was fifteen."

"Why, do you think?" asks Andrea.

"If she worried about hot stoves or choking hazards, she didn't have to worry about what was actually *happening*."

"By overcompensating that way, do you think your mom was helping you?"

I consider that. "No. It made me feel less safe."

I can feel Andrea nodding, tilting her chin, stroking her neck—the way she does when she's letting me connect my own dots.

...

When my daughter is bigger, I will teach her to fight, to take chances, to speak her mind, to jump in the ocean, even. But right now, her skull is baby-bird soft and she can't speak a word, and it is on *me*—the only person in this house who truly gets how dangerous this world is—to keep her alive. So I order every crib mattress Amazon sells to make sure I get the firmest, least-likely-to-suffocate-a-baby one. . . . And place her in her car seat in the dry corner of the shower so I can wash my hair and make sure she's breathing at the same time. . . . And rush her to the pediatrician to make sure the "perfectly normal" (according to Lisa) cyst on her head isn't leukemia. . . . And ask Casey's best friend to cut me a sheet of plywood to slide under the extra-firm crib mattress that still worries me. . . . And buy a label maker so I can mark the breast milk I pump when I'm forced to go on antibiotics for strep throat.

Lisa, my lifeguard, is the only person who can keep my anxiety in check. She grew up in Detroit—in the same housing projects as Diana Ross, she'll proudly tell you—and she's as tough as she is kind, funny, and smart. The original plan was for her to be here at night, while Casey is away filming, so I could sleep better. But I quickly realized I needed more support. Fine, a lot more. What I really need is constant surveillance, someone to spot me if I start to spiral, reel me in from the deeps.

Casey's on his way home for the weekend. "I can't wait to nap with you two," he said on the phone. Nap? Nope. Never mind that Casey's been filming stunts nonstop all week and I'm sleepless and streppy; rest is not on the agenda. We will not be curling up in our fluffy white bed like an organic diaper commercial family today. I've booked a private, weekend-long infant CPR course for Casey and me, and it starts in an hour.

I'm racing around, clearing a dumpster's worth of Amazon packaging from the dining room table, when Lisa says her first What the Fuck of the day.

"Hey, Kim?" she calls. "What the fuck is this?"

Securing Capri in her sling—I like to keep her strapped to my chest so I can feel her heart beating—I zoom into the kitchen to find Lisa staring into my refrigerator at the row of frosty golden baggies I've labeled xxxANTIOBIOTIC MILK!xxx.

Oh, that. It's perfectly explainable. "I'm labeling them so we only give her the tainted milk once a day," I say. "*Only* in the morning, so we can keep an eye out." *In case the milk poisons her.*

Lisa blinks her phoenix eyes, tosses her long braid. "Uh-uh."

I stare back. "What?"

My doula's mouth quivers. She's trying to take me seriously. "We talked about this. Your milk is not tainted. The doctor said it was perfectly fine for her."

"But what if it's not?"

Lisa reaches into the fridge and begins peeling off the labels. "Sorry," she says, all tough love now, "it's just gonna be *milk*."

Usually, when Lisa blows the whistle, I fall into line, relieved that extreme measures won't be necessary, after all; I'm just overreacting again. Last week, after barely an argument, I sent back the two-thousand-dollar heart monitor I'd stress-ordered online. But today, Lisa's sternness undoes me. I wrap my arms around Capri's dreaming body, slump to the kitchen floor, and burst into tears.

"You always say trust my instincts," I sniffle. "But how—if I don't know what's normal anxiety and what's not?"

Lisa closes the refrigerator, crouches next to me, rubs my back. "As long you're doing no harm to your baby," she says, "whatever you do is okay. I'm just trying to make your life easier."

"And you do." I curl into her arms. "How will I do this when you're gone?"

I once told Casey, when he dared to mention how much we're spending to have a doula around the clock, that I'd spend my savings, happily, for the sense of security Lisa gives me. I know how entitled that sounds. What a different story it would be if I'd gotten pregnant in my twenties, when I could barely afford rent, let alone good therapy and a doula. Could I have survived new motherhood then? Plenty of women do, of course. Lots of people grow up with no clue what a normal family looks like and figure out how to create one on their own. I'm increasingly sure I'm not one of those people. I need Lisa to guide me, but she won't be here forever.

"Listen to me, Kim." Lisa crosses her legs to face me. "You're a strong, badass woman, and you're going to be a strong, bad-ass mom. You'll teach yourself, like you always have."

My conversations with Lisa have grown to be about much more than the practicalities of baby care and mothering. We talk about our fears, our failures and favorite things, in long conversations that have stitched us close. I understand how she became the tender, bossy, super-doula she is today, and Lisa gets why I'm . . . the way I am. She knows what Mom and Aunt Pat and I have been through, separately and to-gether. How I got herpes. Why my natural state is high alert.

I've taken Lisa back in time to Earle Avenue, Hewlett Point, the Ailey School, Club Shelter, and even the Midtown strip club, where I hit my rock bottom. Even so, even know-ing where I come from, Lisa believes I'm going to be a badass mom. Her vote of confidence gives me courage.

Maybe she's right, I think, as I pull my waking, wriggling baby from her sling. Maybe I can figure this out. Learn to be a mother like I learned to laugh, dance, open up, look up, fight for myself. Not by studying books, but by studying the people I admire.

Even in my weakest moments, I've found the strength (and it takes a lot of it) to reach out for help and guidance. That's one reason I'm still here.

...

I didn't expect to miss my job when I became a mom. I imagined spending at least a year with Capri strapped to my chest. Heartbeat to heartbeat, we'd take long walks around the canyon, practice our breakdancing moves, and slowly, naturally, get me back to the "5'9", 125" I so boldly printed on my résumé in the days before I hid the scale and began eating for two.

But my daughter is only two months old when I start feeling edgy. I don't like being financially reliant on my husband. To be dependent on another person, even the person I've learned to trust most in the world, doesn't feel safe. So when Casey books a job coordinating stunts for a new Marvel TV show and asks if I want to double Hayley Atwell, I say yes.

With only a month to *Agent Carter* and twenty pounds to Hayley, my new-mom anxiety shape-shifts, lightning-fast, into weight anxiety. Sure, my body is providing sustenance for Capri, but that isn't enough to justify arm cellulite. Now that I'm no longer sheltering someone inside of me, the self-acceptance and body positivity that pregnancy gifted have gone out the window. I dig my scale out of the bathroom cabinet, book a crash course with Charlie, and start eating for half a person. Five days a week, I drag Lisa and Capri to the tae kwon do studio, where the punching bag stands in for my new worst enemy, Post-Baby Body.

When I can't pummel PBB into submission, I eat for a quarter of a person, work out for three. I have to be all things now: a good mom, a good wife, a size 4 successful stuntwoman—but not too successful. I can't go back to filming dozens of projects every year. I have to find just the right balance, for Capri.

Episode one of *Agent Carter* turns out to be a touch demanding. On the first day, I hop a six-foot fence, land with a loud *snap*, walk it off, and do some more damage to my right ankle with two more takes. The urgent care doctor says child-birth makes your ligaments extra-loose and prone to tearing, like mine did—who knew? But the pain is familiar, and I've already rehearsed the rest of the episode, so I decide to finish the job. After a weekend of rest, I wrap the hell out of my ankle, stuff myself into a too-tight pencil skirt and a pair of heels, climb on top of a pickup truck, and do what I have to do.

No, I do more than I have to. I fight my ass off on top of that moving truck. I float above my torn ligaments and sleep-lessness, and I crush it. Driving home from set with Casey—ankle icing on the dash, the hot San Pedro wind in my hair, and my breast pump wheezing away—I feel just the right amount of successful.

Then, after a heavenly hot shower, I weigh myself.

Seeing the number, I hop off of the scale with my good foot, drop my towel, step back on. The verdict that flickers to the surface is 147, the same as ten seconds ago, but two pounds greater than yesterday. This enrages me. After every-thing I've put my body through, the number is bigger? Fuck that.

Pulling on a robe, I grab the scale, throw open the French doors, and limp into the night. At the edge of the lawn, I smash the scale on the garden wall, cracking it down the middle.

"We're done," I say to the pieces in my hands.

I know it's not that easy. I'll still have body issues tomor-row, maybe forever. The world will present new ways for me to judge, rate, and punish myself. But I mean it when I say I'm done with all the weighing. If Dad was here, he'd call me a drama queen—and fine, he'd be a little bit right. But my grand gesture was for me, nobody else.

Next time I'm in a fog, calculating calories or slipping away from the table to repent for a big, healthy meal, I'll remember this promise: *Never again will I let a number tell me how I should feel about myself.*

The scale is broken, but I'm not.

21

THIS IS
WHERE I
LEAVE YOU

2014
Thirty-seven years old

A few years ago, around the time she changed the spelling of her name to Pat-Tree-Sha, Aunt Pat wrote an open letter to the whole Tyler family. It was a good letter, truthful and raw and right on the mark about the destructive attitudes and coping mechanisms that plagued us. I was grateful that she'd written it; for once I wasn't the only one calling us out. But I remember thinking this couldn't have been written by Aunt Pat, who always spoke her truth but refrained from critiquing others. It was a long letter, mostly clear and incisive, but rambling and confusing in places. This is what would be left if you cut away the tangled parts and left the seed of it:

My dear Family,

This is a long time in coming. I have wanted to write to everyone for many years now. Today is the day.

I have been watching, searching, and deeply looking at all my parts for many years now. I also needed to look at us as a family. I see many things: love, compassion, strength, creativity, loyalty, and patterning. We are all patterning our lives on our parents', as they did on theirs, and so on. . . .

I sense that alcohol is our mighty suppressor. It keeps us away from the truth of who we are, it keeps us in the chains of slavery, so we don't make waves or question, or if we do, we rationalize our truths away. "We can work it out, it will be better tomorrow, I was only pulling up the covers." We sweep all the real truths under the carpet that by now is as big as a house.

Another killer is humor, a common scapegoating technique in dysfunctional families. "Can't you take a joke?" is an oppressive statement. . . . I have used alcohol and I have used humor to keep me from my truth. We all had the same legacy passed to us. THIS MUST STOP AND IT MUST STOP NOW. We must not pass it to the children coming into the world.

I love you all very much,

Pat-Tree-Sha

It wasn't long after writing the letter that Aunt Pat was diagnosed with Alzheimer's. I think she'd had the disease awhile, and we were just in denial—even me, the truth junkie. There had been signs, of course: the missed movie dates with Mom, her front door left wide open through the night, and the new, sometimes jarring, forthrightness in her speech and manner. But Aunt Pat was always a nonconformist, and it was easy, at first, to decide she was just becoming truer to herself with age. Now sixty, she lives in a group home with twenty-four-hour care for people with dementia. She does bodywork on her housemates (who tell Mom she's changed their lives) and goes on all the group outings to parks and museums on the Whistlestop bus. As much as she's changed, she's still Aunt Pat, not feeling the least bit sorry for herself about any of it. But the disease has been accelerating in recent months. It's already harder for her to hold a conversation than it was the last time we spoke on the phone.

Wanting to see her before it gets worse, I've taken a few days off *Agent Carter* to come to Marin—just in time, what do you know, for Aunt Kristy's Fourth of July tiki party.

Collette and I sit on Kristy's living room sofa, bouncing our babies (Collette's daughter is just seven months older than Capri, now three months) and clapping for Aunt Pat as she shimmies across the carpet in the loose linen pantsuit Mom picked out for her. I don't think Aunt Pat is concerned about our family's drinking habits anymore. She doesn't seem the least bit interested in what's going on out there.

Through the sliding doors, cousins, nieces, nephews, aunts, and uncles splash in the pool, laugh around the barbecue, and get down to Rhianna. I like our party better, too—just the five of us and the strictly sixties playlist Collette made for Aunt Pat. Music from her youth keeps Aunt Pat happy and calm—not her default mode anymore, sadly.

As the playlist downshifts from "The Twist" to the Turtles' "Happy Together," Aunt Pat sways over to us, reaching out her magic hands. "May I hold a niece?"

I put my hand on my sister's. "She can hold Capri; she hasn't yet."

I settle my daughter into Aunt Pat's arms, staying close in case Aunt Pat forgets she's holding a baby, which seems possible.

It's hard not to be sad that Capri will never know the Aunt Pat I know, the quiet warrior somewhere inside the sweet, doddering woman with us now. But if Capri can't know my mentor in person, I will let my life and actions be lit by Aunt Pat's example. That might be the only part of motherhood I get right, but here's to the hope it will make up for the rest.

"I brought you something," I say over the Supremes, digging into the pocket of my suffocatingly tight, pre-pregnancy jeans. "Do you remember this?" I hold up the amethyst pendant Aunt Pat gave me when I was thirteen.

But she only has eyes for Capri. "*Mmm*," she says, turning a slow circle with my daughter.

"It has healing powers," I say, shadowing them. "I feel better when I wear it. Do you want to keep it for a while?"

"Yes," she says, simply.

I'm clasping the chain around her neck when Aunt Kristy approaches in short shorts and a plunging neckline, sexy as ever. You'd never know they were sisters, and not just because Grandma Gen's "Kristy-Kristy Baby Doll" is twenty years younger than Aunt Pat. If Aunt Pat is like a soft blanket, comforting and warm, Aunt Kristy is like a lit match—fiery but, I think, also vulnerable. She lived alone with them in the house at Earle Avenue for seven years after Mom and Aunt Daphne left home. I sometimes want to ask her what that was like, but I think I'd only get burned.

"You haven't said hello to me yet!" She hugs me.

"Sorry!" I say. "It's just so smoky out, I wanted to get Capri straight inside."

There are forest fires again. This time in the Sierras, close enough for the pollution to carry on the wind. But even on the clearest day, I wouldn't be in that garden. Grandma Gen is out there, reclining on a lounge chair. I haven't seen or talked to her since the big blowout, a choice I silently affirmed as I passed her on my way in and saw his ring glinting in her cleavage.

"Oh, of course!" says Aunt Kristy. She makes a show of admiring Capri. "Did I hear your mama fell off a *truck* playing a superhero?!" she says, squeezing a chubby leg.

"Something like that," I say.

"Well, I think you're a superhero for going back to work so soon," says Kristy.

"Thank you," I say. Kristy's never been one to gush. I wonder what she wants.

"So Grandma Gen asked if she could have a picture with Capri?"

And there it is.

Exchanging a look with Collette, I carefully wrest my child back from Aunt Pat. Holding Capri tight, I try to sync my breath with hers, hot and whispery on my collarbone. *In through the nose, out through the mouth.* The last time I had to deal with Grandma Gen, I acted from pure impulse and adrenaline. I had no tools for handling a conversation like that. I have tools now—what are they again? I press my thumb to the BTC tattoo on my wrist, my jackrabbiting pulse. Over my dead body will I hand my baby to that predator. She'll never get to hold her perfect great-granddaughter like a trophy.

Aunt Kristy cocks her head, awaiting my response.

"Sorry," I say, "but—"

Hold on. Why am I apologizing? I've been working on this; I know why I say sorry for every damn thing. It's because deep down I blame myself for what he did. I also blame myself for causing my family pain by stirring the pot and making them look at the reality of our past. My sorriness is stored in my bones. I want it out.

"Kristy," I say, the strength of my voice surprising me, "you can tell Grandma Gen I said no."

One reason I love my job so much is that for all the beatings I take, I sometimes get to be the avenger, rising up to kick the oppressor's ass—and on a really good day, kill him. But that kind of fighting has never given me a rush like the one I have walking out of Kristy's party. My goodbyes said to the people who matter, I carry my sleeping baby down the tiki-lined garden path—eyes ahead past Grandma Gen—and up the sloping driveway to my parked rental car.

The sky is darkening as I bundle Capri into the car. When she's safe and secure, I slide into the driver's seat, releasing the top button of my jeans with a sigh.

Checking in with myself in the rearview mirror, I'm surprised by what I see: a fighter, a mother, a woman I understand. For the first time in my life, I don't wish for someone better; I'm good with the person who's here now—me.

"This is the last family party you'll ever go to," I tell myself.

I said this at Kristy's last party, too, but I must not have been ready yet. It was last Thanksgiving, and I was pregnant. Casey and I were the only ones not drinking, which was a new perspective for me. Most everyone else was doing exactly what Aunt Pat described in her letter: getting drunk, cracking jokes, dancing, and being in denial about how fucked up we were. Without a glass of wine to numb myself to the mania, I was one big exposed nerve by the time Aunt Daphne cornered me and started defending him: "It's just so hard for me to wrap my head around my father being seen in such an awful way," she said, her soft voice quaking. "He was just so wonderful in our eyes; he could do no wrong."

Just breathe. Poor, kind Aunt Daphne. I gathered myself and told her I understood, which wasn't true, but I did feel compassion for her—for all of them, as annoying as they were.

Every one of us is surviving the best we know how.

...

I used to say I couldn't wait for this part of my life—the healing part—to be over. I thought one day I'd wake up all better, and never have to carry the weight of what happened to me again. But I'm starting to understand that's not how it works. When you've lived through abuse, you *can* grow up to find true love and success beyond your wildest dreams, but that doesn't mean the work is done. As Aunt Pat wrote in my favorite poem, "we are all masterpieces, painted over repeatedly"—while our original paint, and our original pain, remains, under it all.

So I'll get my black belt one day. I'll keep my body strong enough to fight to the death, if I need to. But I won't expect to conquer my deepest fear, that something will happen to Capri. I'll have to learn to live with that, while somehow not letting her feel it. Just like I'll have to work not to pass along my phobias of the ocean, dark windows, showers, small bathrooms, and all the others. I might have to live with flashbacks for the rest of my life, too, though they're so much rarer now.

But my point is, all of this is doable, because I choose life, and this is life. Aunt Pat always taught me that everything is a choice. You can choose the angle from which to approach your challenges, your decisions, your opportunities, your fights. Each day I wake up and choose to be the best mom I can, to protect my daughter as best I can, to create the healthiest family I can.

We can also choose how we identify ourselves. Once, I identified as a victim. As I got stronger, I was supposed to call myself a survivor. But the label felt too neat and tidy, too final. I didn't just survive what he did, I thrived. And there's still so much more to become.

EPILOGUE

To write this book, I took a deep dive back into therapy, sometimes Zooming with Andrea three times a week. Seeing my story laid out on paper brought some painful realizations into sharp focus: how neglected and abused I'd been; how little help had been available to me. As I wrote and rewrote, excavating the narrative that felt most truthful, I realized that for all the work I'd done to make peace with myself in the now, I hadn't made peace with my child self. I still felt anger toward her for not fighting harder, not speaking up.

One day in therapy, Andrea asked if I was familiar with the work of Gabor Maté, MD, a physician and author with a groundbreaking take on trauma. (I was not, but that's what YouTube is for.) As I watched video after video, Dr. Maté's message was clear: if we don't deal with our trauma, it will manifest in our bodies as disease, depression, or both. I thought of Mom's heavy steel box, Dad's shadow enemies, my lifetime of disordered eating, and especially Aunt Pat's Alzheimer's. Each of us, in our own way, was proving Dr. Maté's theory. Maybe he had answers for us—or at least for me, the one asking the questions.

I sent a direct message to Dr. Maté's Instagram account, as well as to his son's, introducing myself. (I realize this sounds stalkerish, but I promise I was very polite and normal about it.) To my amazement, I was soon face-to-face with Dr. Maté on Zoom. I've worked with numerous celebrities as a stunt-woman and don't tend to get starstruck, but this was different. Here was a renowned doctor, author, and activist who immediately took time out of his day to connect with a stranger. I was humbled.

During our powerful conversation, Dr. Maté said something I'd never heard in all my years of therapy: that my deepest trauma was not my abuse. "Before you were sexually abused," he told me, "you were cut off from adults and nurturing. The abuser knows with a laser light who they can perpetrate on; they sense when a child has a lack of protection. That does not mean the child wants it, deserves it, or in any way invites it. It means the bully can always sense the vulnerability of the victim. That lack of protection from your parents was what allowed the whole thing to happen. And *that* was your primary trauma."

The news blew me backward. Here I was, writing a book about my sexual abuse, as my seven-year-old daughter went about her carefree life, as safe and protected as any child can ever be. When I was her age, I'd never known safety. Of course that must have traumatized me.

Dr. Maté asked if I'd ever been treated with psychedelics. I told him I'd taken ecstasy back in my club days, and it hadn't helped me to move forward, only to temporarily forget. "Not really my cup of tea," I said, dismissing the idea.

As we signed off, he suggested I check out a documentary he'd done called *The Wisdom of Trauma*. I did, of course. The documentary looks at the connection between trauma, illness, addiction, and society. Near the end, a cancer patient heals his life with psychedelic therapy. Witnessing the man's transformation, his newfound peace, I started to rethink the idea of doing it myself.

While widely illegal today, the therapeutic use of MDMA and psilocybin, a hallucinogen found in certain mushrooms, may soon be legal throughout the United States (a handful of cities and states have already decriminalized magic mushrooms outright). Experts project FDA approval for these breakthrough treatments within the next two years, and the data tells us it's time. One study, published in *Nature Medicine* in 2021, showed that two months after treatment, 67 percent of subjects who received MDMA therapy were PTSD-symptom-free, compared with 32 percent who received a placebo with therapy. Meanwhile, ketamine is legal for therapeutic use by registered practitioners, and studies on the therapeutic use of other banned psychedelics are promising as well.

Once I'd done my research and decided to take the leap into psychedelic therapy, Dr. Maté connected me with a practicing doctor in Los Angeles, who led me through two preparation sessions, where we discussed my past and what I was hoping to get from the experience. She decided that MDMA (otherwise known as ecstasy) would be the most effective "medicine" for me. As the doctor explained, most pharmaceuticals prescribed for PTSD are designed to manage symptoms, but not deal with what is underlying them. MDMA combined with therapy helps create a sense of safety within which the brain may revisit and reframe disturbing memories with self-compassion. If anything could help me mend my troubled relationship with Little Kimberly, I thought this might be it.

Words can't do justice to my experience with MDMA therapy. It was just too profound to fully capture in language. But with help from the doctor's notes (interspersed below), I'll attempt to describe the psychedelic "journeys" that would revolutionize my life.

Process notes: Kimberly Shannon Murphy, Journey #1,
February 25, 2022
   At 10:30, 135 milligrams

At the beginning of the session, I set my intention: *Help me connect with my little one.*

The doctor and I settled into my living room, where I created an altar with flowers, crystals, and pictures of Aunt Pat, Casey, and Capri.

The medicine took its time to kick in. Did I want to wear a sleep mask? asked the doctor. Perched on the edge of my sofa, gripping Aunt Pat's amethyst, I shook my head. Too scary. I was on high alert, wondering how I'd respond. Would I try to dance on the countertops, run and dive into the pool? This turned out not to be a concern. As the MDMA started to work, my anxiety melted. Sinking into the pillows, I closed my eyes. Soon, as if in a dream, my little one appeared, wearing her burgundy velvet Christmas dress. Her head was scraped and her knees were bleeding, but she wasn't sad, she was smiling.

My little one stood alone in the silent redwood grove near Aunt Pat's house in Marin. She held out her hand, and I tried to take it but couldn't reach. I told the doctor, who guided me through some exercises until I was finally able to grasp Little Kimberly's hand. Still, I couldn't follow when she turned up the trail. I couldn't move. I felt stuck in cement.

The doctor suggested we try sitting awhile. I lowered myself into some tall grass at the side of the trail, and the little one climbed into my lap, snuggling close.

I began to cry. "I'm sorry I've left you alone for so long," I told her. "I'm sorry you're still wearing that stupid dress."

My little one shrugged. "I don't mind it," she said cheerfully. "It doesn't define me. It's just a dress."

But the dress and the blood bothered *me*, so the doctor suggested I change the little one and clean her up.

I did. That was better.

For several hours, you alternated between talking to me and processing with your little girl.

You visited her on her communion day, then gave her the opportunity to unburden any beliefs or feelings she held from that day.

I think my little one took me back to our communion day to help me release my shame. I'd never realized, before, how much of it I carried. The doctor suggested I pick an element— wind, light, water, or fire—to help clear it away. I chose fire, but my little one said, "No, we can't start a fire in a forest." So I asked for water instead. As the request left my lips, water flooded over us. I imagined his handprints washing away from our bodies as we lay side by side, holding hands.

When the water was gone, I was able to stand and walk up the trail with my little one. As I held her tiny hand in mine, she looked up at me, beaming.

"What took you so long?" she asked.

In that moment, I was struck with an overpowering realization: it was always her, guiding me from within. *She* was my glimmer, the light inside me that refused to go out, no matter how bad things got. Over and over again, she'd saved me.

Now it was my turn to save her.

"How can I help you?" I asked. "What do you need?"

My little one said there was more that she needed to show me, on another day. It was late afternoon. The booster dose of medicine was wearing off. The doctor gave me electrolytes, fruit, and Advil, and we all sat quietly for a while.

When I left my little one, she was sitting happily in the forest in her clean clothes. The last words I remember her saying were, "You know this is what we're here for, right? This is what we're supposed to do with all of this. It's why we were born."

Process notes: Kimberly Shannon Murphy, Journey #2, April 30, 2022
   At 10:30, 135 milligrams

My intention for my second journey was to witness whatever my little one still needed to show me. I began the session
by letting her know it was safe to unburden herself now. I
was ready and available to see what she wanted to show me.
I laid out pictures of family members—Mom, Dad, Collette,
Grandma Gen, and him.

Soon, we were in the basement at Earle Avenue. Music
and laughter came from upstairs. It was the year Mom inter-
rupted him.

He was straddling me on the bar. I was kicking, twisting,
punching—fighting!

How wrong I'd been about my little one. How brave she was.
But bravery wasn't enough.

When Mom cracked the basement door, he was kneeling on
my hands, holding a pillow over my face, nearly smothering me.

At 1:25, you started to kick your legs. You said, "I hate you.
I hate you." You sat up with your hand around your throat,
making choking noises.
  You asked me to tell you you were safe. I said that you were.
  You said, "I couldn't breathe. He didn't care if I died."

At 2:40, you asked for a picture of your child self. You lay
back down with the picture on your heart, telling her, "That
was no game. Thank you for telling me. You shouldn't have
had to carry that for so long."

I'd never been fully able to explain the undercurrent of fear
that ran through my life. Now that I realized how violent

he was—how he'd robbed me of my hands, my breath—it was like a light had switched on, I understood so much. No wonder my little one had been afraid to cross him. No wonder death had always felt *this close* to me. Even my phobia of open water made a new kind of sense. My abuser was all-powerful; so was the ocean.

On MDMA, with guidance, I was given access to my scariest memories, as well as the capacity to process them without being overcome. Vivid and graphic as they were, the memories didn't pull me down because I understood I was safe now. He was no longer a threat; I didn't need to survive him because I already had.

What I did need, true to my bulimic tendencies, was a good purge. I needed him out of my body.

"Could I have a bowl, please?" I asked the doctor.

The rest was less polite. After spitting into the bowl a few times, I asked for a second bowl, filled with water, and a picture of Grandma Gen and him. I tore the image into the tiniest pieces, threw them in the water, and spat on them for good measure. But I didn't like seeing parts of my abusers floating in the bowl, so I fished them out, wrapped them in a towel, put the bundle in the water, and covered it with a rock.

Satisfied, I turned to the doctor. "Can I scream?"

She thought this was such a great idea, she joined me.

"IT'S OVER. . . . IT'S OVER. . . . IT'S OVER!" we shouted at the top of our lungs.

I was ready to leave the basement for good.

The doctor said to make sure I took my little one with me,

but I didn't need reminding. We climbed the stairs, together as one.

I won't leave my little one behind again. Not that she'd let me. After my second journey, she stayed close. Sometimes, in the shower, I'd look down and see her tiny feet. At first, I was rattled. *"Is this normal?"* I wrote to Dr. Maté. He replied that it was. Now that I'd connected with my inner child, she was more likely to show herself to me. She trusted me, and at last, I trusted her. I began to listen to her needs and apply them to my adult life. Truth, boundaries—everything she was missing, I can provide for us now.

Accessing my most painful memories from a place of safety and power has allowed me to see myself in a new way. I have the strength to walk away from situations and people who aren't loving, every time—including people I love very much.

Though I omitted most of them from the book, some of my family members remain critical of my decision to publicly share my story. The process of writing *around* them has forced me to examine the roles some of them played in my abuse: by turning the other cheek, by excusing him, by suggesting I should just shut up and get over it, they were complicit, and they continue to be to this day. Many of our wounds remain unhealed.

I'm coming to terms with that.

This new acceptance began with my third MDMA journey, the last I'll take for now, but probably not forever. My little one and I have become integrated into my adult body, but retain our unique perspectives. Together, we returned to the house at Earle Avenue. First, we folded our torturer in half and put him in the fireplace (it was the logical thing to do). "Come on, everybody," I said to the rest of my family, "let's get out of this place!" But nobody heard me. My sister stuck herself to a wall, and hard as I tried, I couldn't peel her off.

"They're not ready," said my little one. "They have to decide for themselves."

As always, she was right.

...

While I've surrendered any illusions that most of my family, including my dad and my sister, will ever walk with me on this journey, I live my life in honor of the family member who unfailingly did. Some months ago—following Grandma Gen's passing by six years—Aunt Pat succumbed to Alzheimer's at the Fresno Veterans Affairs Medical Center, where she'd lived out her final years unburdened by the weight of her memories, and ours. My loving mentor is gone, but her spirit glimmers on in my heart, reminding me to *just breathe*. And always speak my truth.

ACKNOWLEDGMENTS

I want to first thank my mother, Kathy Murphy, who had every reason to be terrified of our story being told to the world, but supported me anyway and stood by my side, all the way through. I know how hard this was for you, Mom. Thank you for being brave. I'm sorry he took so much from you, and I hope this book will help you, too, take all of yourself back. I look forward to continuing our work together, healing together, and making our relationship stronger every day.

I want to thank my Aunt Pat. Without you, I wouldn't be the woman I am today and wouldn't have had the courage to write this book. You must have felt as if you were drowning in a sea of pain, all our pain, all those years. We did it, we finished telling the story you had the courage to start telling in 1952. May you rest in POWER, Aunt Pat. For anyone who feels like they can't possibly make a difference in someone's life, my Aunt Pat is proof that you can.

I would like to thank every extended family member who spoke to me about their experiences and helped me understand my pain better. I will forever be in your corner. We are safe now.

I want to thank my amazing husband, Casey O'Neill, who

has been with me every step of the way on my book journey, holding my hand and reminding me, even on my weakest days: "You can do this." Casey, you are my rock. I'm so lucky to be your wife and share this life with you.

I want to thank my daughter, Capri, who has taught me more in her eight years of life than anyone ever has. You are a light in my darkness, Capri. The spirit that lives inside you is a gift. I am so blessed to call you mine and be your mama, and I can't wait to see what you do with your life. I hope I can give you all the things I never had in every way. Thank you for choosing me. I promise to make you proud every day I am on this earth.

I want to thank Cameron Diaz. Cameron, your unwavering support through all the late-night phone calls and all my tears helped me create this. Thank you for your beautiful foreword—I'm still pinching myself. I love you, lady.

I want to thank the two people who gave me the biggest starts in my career, Chris Harrison and George Aguilar. Thank you for seeing something special in me. I want to thank Timmy Regisford for giving me his blessing to tell our story. Although he might be a small part of the book, he has been a big part of my life, supporting me in all my endeavors, showing me my potential, and believing in me when I did not believe in myself.

I want to thank Serge Aly, who took me into his home when I did not have one, for being my very best friend and someone who I always could look up to.

I want to thank my Girl and Boy Gang. These women and men, the past two years, have listened to me over and over again, on the phone, in their kitchens on FaceTime, in person, you name it. They have supported me beyond my wildest dreams and I love them all dearly: Michele Cavanagh Belvedere, Maryann Kemp Troy, Lucy Fry, Lona Vigi, Leanna Nausha, Sheree Mackee, Kim Reddick, Jesse Lutz, Yarrow Lutz, Robin Fredricks, Jamie Tyler, Lee-Anne Jennings, Zoë Bell, Megan Hubbell, Holly Pack, Kaitlin Olson, Dani Ruah, Zach Duhame, Jai Courtney, Chelsea Bacon, Mark Fichera, and Cameron, again.

I would like to thank Charlie Shin, who not only pushed me in all the good ways to receive my black belt but has become one of my closest friends. Charlie: you have taught me so much more than how to perfect my side kick. You are a friend for life.

I want to thank Kaitlin Olson for reading my audiobook. As much as this was a painful story to write, I knew it would be too hard for me to read aloud, and no one could do it better than you, Kaitlin. I'll never forget your text to me after reading the book: "Whatever you need, I got you, just tell me the time and the place." I love you, K.O.

I want to thank all the women behind the scenes that made this book what it is. My incredible ghostwriter, Genevieve Field. Our endless phone calls, emails, trips . . . You know more about my life than anyone on this planet—possibly including me. Your ability to put my words on paper in such a beautiful way has made this book what it is: a painful story, full of hope. And thanks to Lauren Smith Brody of The Fifth Trimester for introducing us. My agent, Nicki Richesin, who believed in me and my story before any publisher did, and fights for me every step of the way. Julie Will, my editor at Harper Wave: you are incredible. You saw a diamond in the sand, and I could not be more grateful. I want to thank Susan Efros, who, twenty years ago, read my work, edited it, and poured herself into me and my story. I love you, Susan. All these years later, I finished what we started.

I would like to thank Dr. Gabor Maté, Dr. Bruce Perry, Dr. Nicole LePera, and Dr. Richard Schwartz, who took the time to read this book and put their support behind it. I will be forever grateful.

I would like to thank my lifelong therapist, Andrea Spiritos, who gave me priceless survival tools and who always, happily, was on call for me when I needed her. Thank you, Andrea, for all your words of wisdom, for never making me feel crazy, and for giving me a safe space in which to feel and heal. I'll be forever grateful for you and all you've done for me.

I would like to thank the doctor who did my psychedelic journeys with me. You know who you are, and you changed my life.

Finally, I would like to thank *myself* for pushing through this project and never giving up. Some days, that meant writing through tears, then picking myself up off the floor to go to work and jump off a building—or whatever it was that day.

This book was forged from tears, pain, and struggle. May it remind you, dear reader: No matter how challenging things may be, you got this.

ABOUT THE AUTHOR

KIMBERLY SHANNON MURPHY is a leading Hollywood stuntwoman who has performed in more than 130 feature films and television shows, including *Top Gun: Maverick, Once Upon a Time in Hollywood, Captain America, The Tomorrow War, Bright, The Eternals, The Old Guard, Bird Box, The Hunger Games, The Lone Ranger, Salt, Enchanted, Marvel's Agent Carter, Euphoria, Big Little Lies, The Mick,* and *Westworld.* She has doubled numerous A-list actresses, including Cameron Diaz, Charlize Theron, Blake Lively, Angelina Jolie, Taylor Swift, Yvonne Strahovski, Hayley Atwell, Sandra Bullock, and Uma Thurman. As an actor, Kimberly has appeared in *Nash Bridges: The Movie, Curb Your Enthusiasm, NCIS,* and *Criminal Minds,* among others. Since 2018, she has also worked as a stunt coordinator.

A tae kwon do black belt, Kimberly received the 2020 Taurus World Stunt Award for Best Fight in *Once Upon a Time in Hollywood.* She is a two-time Screen Actors Guild Award winner for Best Stunt Ensemble and has been recognized with numerous award nominations, including: the MTV Movie Award for Best Fight in *My Super Ex-Girlfriend,* doubling Uma Thurman; multiple Taurus World Awards in the categories of Best Fight, Best Overall Stunt by a Stunt Woman, and Hardest Hit; and the Action Icon Award for Stuntwoman of the Year.

Kimberly lives in Los Angeles with her husband, the second unit director and stunt coordinator Casey O'Neill, and their daughter, Capri.